Becoming Posthumous

Becoming Posthumous

Life and Death in Literary and Cultural Studies

Jeremy Tambling

Edinburgh University Press

This book is for Pauline

© Jeremy Tambling, 2001
Edinburgh University Press Ltd
22 George Square, Edinburgh

Typeset in New Baskerville by
Palimpsest Book Production Limited,
Polmont, Stirlingshire and
printed and bound in Great Britain by
MPG Books Ltd, Bodmin

A CIP Record for this book is available
from the British Library

ISBN 0 7486 1477 X (paperback)

Contents

Preface

I BEGAN WRITING THIS book with the intention that it should all
read as one essay with breaks for the reader to pause. The
breaks still survive in the way the chapters are set out, but of
course the project has not ended up like this, and the reader
can, of course, and in any case, take it any way she chooses; one
way being to take it as four meditations on 'becoming posthumous' derived from studying *Cymbeline, David Copperfield,*
Nietzsche, and especially his *Ecce Homo,* and Benjamin's 'Theses
on the Philosophy of History.' That would mean dipping at will
into any of the main four parts of the book, and I hope that
Shakespearians, Dickensians, Nietzscheans and Benjaminians will
feel free to do that, leaving out the Introduction if they want to,
and that they will all find something that interests them in their
own or in other sections.

However, the argument is also cumulative, and the Introduction
and the 'Afterlife' sections relate it all to issues of contemporary
culture and to where literary and cultural studies are today, and
to the particular question how to relate to texts of the past, and
to history. Obviously I know about alternative histories, and
counter-memories as these apply in terms of women's histories,
or with race, or colonialism, or gender or class; and 'brushing
history against the grain' is Benjamin's topic and I do not neglect
it, but since the forgetting of history and the loss of memory
became a contentious topic in postmodernism in the 1980s, and

since globalisation, the 'new' topic of the 1990s, is often seen as likely to leave out local histories, there seems a case for going back to those issues. Since in universities there is a current polarisation between those departments which teach canonical or traditional texts and those which reject them, a break which is continued within departments too, I focus here on how or whether we can take the past, or whether it is there to be ignored. I hope some readers will have the desire to read it right through for that interest and for the discussions I offer of the posthumous, and the examples I provide of it.

Teaching texts, too, has become controversial in an atmosphere which looks to culture rather than a specific and ennobled form of that culture – literature, which, being discussed as though formalistically seems to gain a special and ahistorical attention setting it apart from other forms of culture, and from cultural studies or media studies. Attention to the question of speed and to the kind of distracted attention which is required in reading film – the most pervasive cultural form of the twentieth century, and quite confusing the categories of 'culture', popular and non-popular – how can that new form of attention relate to the form of reading required in, say, going through a Victorian novel? Which kind of skill should students be led towards, and does one skill imply a break with the other? And if globalisation is a new issue, and presents a new challenge to describe it, can a text from the past help here? Is not going back into the seventeenth century, for instance, an evasion of the challenge the present offers?

These are, paradoxically, old questions now, but what should happen to the study of literature – which again, divides universities and departments – is inseparable from questions posed in studying history. The response I have had here to these questions has been to work with the trope of the 'posthumous'. F. R. Leavis, in *Revaluation* (1936), once suggested that we read Donne 'as we read the living', the way he said Milton could not be read, but this actually presupposes the posthumous as Donne is certainly among the dead white poets, and Leavis's prescription assumes raising him up to a new status beyond the tomb. The opposite position seems to be put with Stephen Greenblatt beginning *Shakespearean Negotiations* (1988) by saying that what prompted the book was 'the desire to speak with the dead'. The aim is worthy, except that it puts the New Historicist on the side of life versus a dead past, and I have, rather, worked with the assumption that it is not easy to decide what is living and what is not. How should we read the living – let alone the dead? It might be better if we started with the assumption of death working through the living, and not dissociated, therefore, from our sense of the present. My readings are, therefore, examples offered of how looking at literature of the past – which cannot be easily assimilated into a cultural studies whose emphasis is on the present – might still be possible; not that *Becoming Posthumous* accepts the past/present distinction that this implies.

I am grateful to the enthusiasm of people – especially graduate students – who heard the material at its beginning as a seminar paper in the Department of Comparative Literature in the University of Hong Kong; to my colleague Dr Q. S. Tong who helped me understand the ambiguities of my two first titles, *Being Posthumous* and *Becoming Posthumous*, to Wimal Dissanayake, who is not to be blamed for my not including discussion of the pseudonymous as an example of the posthumous, despite his urging me, to Ackbar Abbas, and to Dave Clark, who urged me to write something like this, though perhaps not this, to Chris Barlow, to Ho Cheuk Wing as a research assistant, to the Hong Kong students who heard me lecture on Nietzsche while I was trying to write the part which is included here on him (which no doubt made my lecture comments all the more difficult to follow), and to Edinburgh University Press and Jackie Jones for being so positive about this project so quickly.

Introduction

The End/s of History

1

I N PRESENT-DAY LITERARY and cultural studies, what justifies our looking at texts of the past? Is it easier to read texts of the past, or to read the present? And is the past/present distinction necessary, or immutable, or functional?

In an essay, the Austrian novelist Robert Musil discusses the unease felt about our relation to what has just gone out of fashion, what has recently become the past, in a book which appeared in his lifetime, but which he called *Nachlass zu Lebzeiten*. We can translate this as *Posthumous Papers of a Living Author*:

> What conclusions may we draw from the fact that it is just as ridiculously unpleasant to look at old fashions (so long as they have not yet become costumes), as it is ridiculously unpleasant to look at old pictures, or the outmoded facades of old-style houses, and to read yesterday's books? Clearly . . . that we become unpleasant to ourselves the moment we gain some distance from what we were. This stretch of self-loathing begins several years before now and ends approximately with our grandparents . . . It is only then that what was is no longer outdated, but begins to be old; it is our past, and no longer that which passed away from us . . . the great majority of people would remain surprisingly little moved if, at an advanced age, you were to show them again, in the form of a movie, their grandest gestures and once most stirring scenes.
>
> . . . Art never becomes our past, but always remains that which has passed from us. It is understandable then that we should look back at it every ten or fifteen years with an uneasy eye!

Only great art, that which alone, strictly speaking, merits being called art, constitutes an exception. But the latter has never really fit that well in the society of the living.[1]

Musil in the 1920s reckoned without the power of the nostalgia industry when he wrote as he did of recent fashions, or of art that seems so unimportant twenty-five years later. The nostalgia industry and the pull of 'heritage' gained their power later, in the last thirty years of the twentieth century. Musil notes that 'art exhibits, like the latest fashion, appear in the spring and fall' (79) and comments, in another essay, that if we go by the news and reviews in magazines 'how many deeply moving, prophetic, greatest and very great masters appear in the course of a few months', yet 'a few weeks later hardly anyone can still remember the unforgettable impression they made' ('Surrounded By Poets and Thinkers', *Posthumous Papers*, 74). Their appeal is to be regarded as immediate, accessible; after they go out of time, they die; they do not acquire an afterlife, they never become 'posthumous'. Indeed, to be posthumous is not held to be a compliment. It is an essential aspect of the English national ideology, where signs to Hampshire call it 'Jane Austen's county', and to Dorsetshire 'Hardy country' and Warwickshire 'Shakespeare's county', as part of the national heritage, that these are all outside the category of the posthumous, which is where Robert Musil is, and are held to be immediate, accessible. Shakespeare is accessible, playable in the present-day theatre, intelligible to all alike. The 'posthumous' requires us to think of art as already not quite alive in its own time, hence the implications of Musil's title, or in its afterlife.

2

Musil may point to a break occurring at some point in the last century that now requires the category of the posthumous in which to think about art, or the past, at all. That something has changed is perhaps evident since the revelation of the extent of the Nazi death camps, which Maurice Blanchot called 'an absolute which interrupted history' and about which he said, showing how the power of the event perpetuates itself in its after-life, 'death continues its work'.[2] Blanchot describes posthumous effects, meaning that everything since the death camps is marked by the posthumous; the event offers no possibility of being moved beyond, as with the various suicides, for example, of Paul Celan, Primo Levi, Sarah Kofman, all part of the delayed traumas of the Second World War. This break, which questions the possibility of there being continuity now,[3] articulates with arguments that see in the twentieth century a caesura, to be evidenced in 'end of philosophy' arguments derived from Heidegger in the 1960s, and in such titles as Daniel Bell's *The End of Ideology* (1960) with its sense of 'post-industrial society', or Gianni Vattimo's *The End of Modernity* (1985), or Danto's *The End of Art* or Francis Fukayama's *The End of History and the Last Man* (1992), which intersects with Kojève in the *Introduction to the Reading of Hegel* (1947) on the 'posthistorical'. Amid other forms of the 'post', cyberculture now gives the 'posthuman' and 'posthuman bodies'. The phrases 'the end of art' and 'the end of history' are both Hegelian. The first derives from passages in his *Aesthetics*. Hegel says that 'art, considered in its highest vocation' – by which he means 'the satisfaction of spiritual needs' – 'is, and remains for us, a thing of the past'. And later he says:

> But just as art has its 'before' in nature and the finite spheres of life, so too it has an 'after', i.e. a region which in turn transcends art's way of apprehending and representing the Absolute. For art still has a limit in itself and therefore passes over into higher forms of consciousness. This limitation determines, after all, the position which we are accustomed to assign to art in our contemporary life. For us art counts no longer as the highest mode in which truth fashions an existence for itself . . . We may well hope that art will always rise higher and come to perfection, but the form of art has ceased to be the supreme need of the spirit.[4]

This argument can be taken perhaps as part of the apocalyptic tone which, according to Derrida, has been adopted in philosophy.[5] Earlier periods in Europe thought apocalyptically, as a glance at medieval texts – Dante, *Piers Plowman* – confirms; modernity, premised on time's homogeneity and progression, still produces the apocalypse; Derrida argues that it is indeed the condition of discourse. Let us stay with the possibility that an end has been reached that would make art a thing of the past; it is an archive of another, different moment, and the knowledge that it gives is historical. Its satisfaction cannot now be immediate. It may be compared with Arthur Danto, writing in the 1980s, accepting that decade as the epoch of the 'end of art'. For Danto, art has had a linear history in which it could be taken as meaning the possibility of representation, but there is no more progress to be made in terms of art producing equivalences to perceptual experiences. Artworks will now be produced 'post-historically'.[6] Danto sees this as a liberation. The 'posthistorical' is defined:

> by the lack of a stylistic unity . . . which can be elevated into a criterion and used as a basis for developing a recognitional capacity, and there is in consequence no possibility of a narrative direction.

He associates this with the point that now nothing can fall outside the pale of 'history':

> [T]o say history is over is to say that there is no longer a pale of history for works of art to fall outside of. Everything is possible. Anything can be art. And because the present situation is essentially unstructured, one can no longer fit a master narrative to it.[7]

Following Kojève's 'end of history' argument, comes the work of Arnold Gehlen, who used the term *post-histoire* in 1960 in the then Federal Republic of Germany. His argument is quoted by the postmodern philosopher Gianni Vattimo in *The End of Modernity*. Vattimo defines the 'post-histoire' as

> the condition in which 'progress becomes routine': human capability to order nature through technology has increased . . . [so] that, even while ever-newer achievements have become possible, the increased capability to order and arrange simultaneously makes them ever less 'new' . . . What is new is not in the least 'revolutionary' or subversive; it is what allows things to stay the same.[8]

In *Posthistoire* in 1989, Lutz Niethammer produced a survey of European conservative theorists for whom the concept was relevant, as they saw themselves facing 'anonymous structural processes before which individuals feel . . . powerless' and which they endowed with such properties as 'independence, prominence, dynamism, irreversibility and a capacity to dissolve cultural values'. They were characterised by a melancholia which Niethammer claims Wolf Lepenies makes 'the individualist contrabass of the history of bourgeois society'.[9] In contrast to this, there is Fukuyama's embracing of 'the end of history' first in a paper in 1989, and then in his book with that title. Here, where American-style liberal democracy 'remains the only coherent aspiration that spans different regions and cultures around the globe',[10] there is no room for melancholia. Now that we have arrived at the 'end' of 'socialism', the topic of Derrida in *Spectres of Marx* (1993) – a text which also engages with the theme of 'post-histoire' – there is no other narrative available, no sense that anything remains to be done but to fill in the gaps and complete the existing narrative which was conferred on the nineteenth century by Hegel: that of a single drive towards a complete, homogeneous state.[11]

Danto and Fukuyama offer different views of plenitude and plurality, and their focus is America. They contrast in part with Baudrillard's fascination with America as 'post catastrophe' – so there will be no apocalypse in the future – and asking 'what are you doing after the orgy?'[12] For Baudrillard, everything, including the orgy, is present and accessible now, so when writing about the American present 'when everything is available', Baudrillard argues that a chasm of modernity separates America from Europe, and speaking of himself as European adds 'you are born modern, you do not become so. And we have never become so' (73). Gertrude Stein in 1933 spoke of America as

> the oldest country in the world because . . . America created the twentieth century, and since all the other countries are now living or commencing to be living a twentieth century life, America having begun the creation of the twentieth century in the sixties of the nineteenth century is now the oldest country in the world.[13]

Compare this with Baudrillard calling America 'the only remaining primitive society' (7): the one that has not yet needed to find a history, save in simulacral form – in the repro form of a copy of a copy. The contrast is with Stephen Dedalus, in *Ulysses*, for whom history – personal and Irish, the history of colonisation as well as Irish self-oppression – 'is a nightmare from which I am trying to awake'.[14]

Since the future still looks to be American, the anger that has been caused in French intellectuals about America's status as not needing history (being outside history), and which is mapped out by Jean-Philippe Mathy,[15] has become, as potentially always in Europe when it looks at America, a form of *ressentiment*. This last is the Nietzschean term for envy or rancour, made familiar in Nietzsche's *The Genealogy of Morals*. Lyotard, however, shows the opposite tendency to *ressentiment* in the tendential Americanism of his postmodern 'incredulity towards metanarratives'.[16] But perhaps Lyotard really means incredulity towards narratives: any metanarrative would be metaphysical, definitionally, as an attempt to see an order in events, or someone's hand at work. Incredulity towards metanarratives would be incredulity towards metaphysics, and the idea of 'history' would be part of that.[17] It would be more valid to ask the question, what happens when we think in terms of narratives? Are not all narratives attempts from an outside position to impose order, and so tendentially ideological or metaphysical?[18] If 'the end of history' has been in sight as long as 'history' has been around as an academic subject, in the nineteenth and twentieth centuries, the threat or promise America poses is that such absorption in history is unnecessary: but in that case, are there any advantages in studying history, or in looking at the past?

What remains from statements asserting a qualitative and different structure for the present changed from anything that has gone before, so that previous narratives and models cannot fit, is a severance arguing that that which has passed away is no longer relevant. The question is not how modernity can survive without an attention to history, whatever that history may be, but why anyone should have or need to have that attention, whether it is not a symptom of failure, a failure to let go.

3

Hegel tells us that we have reached something like the end of art in the *Lectures on Aesthetics*, a text published posthumously.

Maurice Blanchot, who among other things worked on putting the *Nachlass* of Nietzsche into French, has commented on how Nietzsche was a victim of 'the inordinate interest we bring to works that come into our possession not by life but by the death of their author'. He continues: 'How strange that the greatest literary glories of our time should be born of entirely posthumous works: Kafka, Simone Weil, Hopkins; or of works partially posthumous, as is the case with Hölderlin, Rimbaud, Lautréamont, Trakl, Musil; and, in an even crueller sense, Nietzsche.' This 'crueller sense' I shall discuss later, in the third part of this book. The posthumous writings gather a fetishised value, as if, in Nietzsche's case, 'they held the very secret and the truth for which he had become mad'.[19] We could add in so many more names: Wittgenstein; Bakhtin; Paul de Man. The posthumous complicates; Hume noted how his *Treatise of Human Nature* 'fell dead-born from the press', which has given its afterlife a ghostly force. In his last sickness, Hume told Adam Smith that the only reason he had for wanting to remain alive was to see the elimination of the strange superstition Christianity, which pervaded the world, yet he doubted that even if he could carry on, Christianity would ever be eliminated. Yet his two essays 'Of Suicide' and 'Of the Immortality of the Soul' – showing that arguments against suicide had no weight, and that the prospect of immortality was without probability – both appeared posthumously, in 1777, as did his *Dialogues Concerning Natural Religion*. These are statements from beyond the tomb which complicate Christianity's life–death distinctions with their own way of asserting an afterlife. How does it affect or how has it constructed our listening to know that Mahler's *Das Lied von der Erde* and his Ninth Symphony – both examples of an *Abschied* – were first heard after Mahler's death? How has our knowledge that E. M. Forster's *Maurice* was deliberately left for posthumous publication shaped our sense of Forster? Yet, alternatively, who knows that Hegel's *Aesthetics* or Saussure's *Course in General Linguistics* are posthumous? They have become part of an undecidability about chronology, an inability to fix any time of the past. The posthumous challenges a life–death distinction and the order in which that distinction is phrased; it throws chronology into disarray, when the works of long dead writers suddenly appear later, out of 'time', and it makes all writing potentially posthumous since it cannot have a punctual relation to a life of writing. I want to propose the posthumous as a way of thinking about the pastness of the past, and about our own present.

Though the present is not as seamless as the idea of the posthistorical (and America as the posthistorical) implies, containing differing times within it, of different cultures and different modes of experiencing time and history, times which vary according to gender, as Julia Kristeva contends in her essay 'Woman's Time', yet it is not obvious exactly why we should give attention to the past and to past texts – and to which past and which past texts? In Frederic Jameson's arguments, the present, as the 'postmodern', is marked by an inability to think critically about the past, by a 'weakening of historicity'. Discussing E. L. Doctorow's *Ragtime*, he says that 'this historical novel can no longer set out to represent the historical past; it can only "represent" our ideas and stereotypes about the past (which thereby at once becomes "pop history")'.[20] The fear of a history that was once so dominating, and the subject of Nietzsche's essay, 'The Uses and Disadvantages of History for Life', whose title says it all, has been replaced, for Jameson, by something else. This is a history which the present has the power to create in the form of nostalgia and heritage, which means the loss of a critique of the present.

To start in the present means beginning, as Walter Benjamin put it, not from 'the good old things, but the bad new ones'.[21] Cultural studies, which has a relationship with the postmodern, has frequently been accused of neglecting history; but what are the claims for the past that it is sometimes claimed that cultural studies ignores?

One influential way of thinking through a relation to the past was T. S. Eliot writing the essay 'Tradition and the Individual Talent' in 1919 on 'tradition', whose awesomeness appears in that it 'cannot be inherited, and if you want it you must obtain it by great labour'. Meaning 'the historical sense, which we may call nearly indispensable to anyone who would continue to be a poet beyond his twenty-fifth year', this requires perception not only of the pastness of the past, but of its presence; the historical sense compels a man to write not merely with his own generation in his bones, but with a feeling that the whole of the literature of Europe from Homer and within it the whole of the literature of his own country has a simultaneous existence and composes a simultaneous order. This historical sense, which is a sense of the timeless as well as the temporal, and of the timeless and the temporal together, is what makes a writer traditional.

Eliot continues by asserting that the contemporary poet has his meaning in relation to 'the dead poets and artists'. He says that 'the necessity that he shall conform, that he shall cohere, is not onesided; what happens when a new work of art is created is something that happens simultaneously to all the works of art which preceded it. The existing monuments form an ideal order among themselves, which is modified by the introduction of the new (the really new) work of art among them.' A third proposition about the contemporary poet emerges in that he 'must be very conscious of the main current, which does not at all flow through the most distinguished reputations. He must be quite aware that . . . art never improves, but that the material of art is never quite the same.'[22]

To put these arguments alongside those of 'the end of art' is instructive: Eliot's assumptions that he can speak for gender and for Europe, *and* can occlude his own American literature in his Eurocentrism, *and* can find a normative age by which poets should change their individual direction make the repeated references to 'the whole' incomplete, and they imply that the poet who wants to open up a relation to the past also represses it. Nor does he question the means by which 'monuments' have become such; choosing to begin with Homer is inert in its acceptance of the order of the ideal order, which is apparently a chronological one, and it pairs with the assumption of a main current, which means that Eliot is only interested in a major literature. Since art never improves (gets better? makes people better?), there is also an apparent political conservatism. These points, which are easy to make, imply a symptomatology of modernism; we could play with Eliot's frequently used word 'order'; but there is another point too: the relationship between tradition and history. Eliot actually is not interested in history. The historical sense, he says, is what makes a writer traditional. Having established that point, he never re-uses the word 'history' in the section but once: 'Shakespeare acquired more essential history from Plutarch than most men could from the whole British Museum . . . The poet must develop or procure the consciousness of the past' (40). Essential history? All you need to know, or the history of essences? The statement's epigrammatic force conceals its assumption, which reveals how little interested in history it is: that the history given in Shakespeare's Plutarch is of the same order as that which (then) modern scholarship might look for.

The distinction between tradition and history, tradition as a reification of history, involves repression and oppression, and carves out a space within the historical for the appearance of an order whose selectivity points to the present investments that Eliot has made, which require such a creation of an ideal order. Eliot's arguments tacitly assume the end of art and are motivated by a fear of that; hence the turning of a historical past into something more authoritarian and uniform: tradition. Eliot's 'tradition' has been challenged by other histories, while it has remained commanding; yet it is worth noting that its position can give no help to those who argue for history as a way of reading the present from the point of view of a different value-system, in an argument which posits that the value of present texts needs to be weighed in relation to our reading of texts of the past. From where do values traditionally/normally appear if not from the past? It is the doubleness of that point which gives Nietzsche's title, 'The Uses and Disadvantages of History for Life' its hold, since values have to do with 'life' as opposed to history. Eliot's proposition that art never improves, though the material of art is never quite the same, aestheticises the past and past texts, and turns their study into formalism – and an equal aestheticism runs through the statement that 'the more perfect the artist, the more completely separate in him will be the man who suffers and the mind which creates' (41). It makes suffering of any kind unrelated to the present, and so to history.

10

4

In the later twentieth century, 'tradition' became 'heritage'. As the 'end of history' and the 'end of art' have been announced, museums for both history and art have proliferated. If the postmodern is the moment of the 'culture of amnesia', for example in the way development has bulldozed cities into wholly new shapes, erasing older patterns and buildings, so it has also made everything a matter for conservation and collectible, greatly increasing the range of museums, and making the museum – a word which nearly rhymes with mausoleum[23] – one of the growth areas in the modern service sector. Three-quarters of the museums in the UK (half of all of which are privately or independently owned) are post-1945.

Yet while the museum may have extended and pluralised cultural memories, in its present-day form it is not so much the entrance into another world, but an extension of the shopping mall and part of 'infotainment'. We can say that the last thirty years or so have witnessed enormous growths in investment in 'the past' and in conservation: the National Trust in Britain, for instance, founded in 1895 and devoted to conserving old country homes (these above all) and other sites, increased its membership from 278,000 in 1971 to two million in 1990. Has this stress on heritage marked a culture of memory (everything must be remembered), or a culture of amnesia? Perhaps the issue should be rephrased by seeing that memory and forgetting are not binary opposites. The installation of memory is also a mode of forgetting, for any memory that is instituted also precludes other memories. What has to be put into the memory is in danger of being forgotten, just as forgetting – repression in Freud's terms – is a form of memory. Forgetting, if that is what the postmodern is good at, is an active process, a putting out of sight. So a culture of amnesia works by memory, and a culture of memory, which is encouraged by a stress on heritage, disadvantages present-day thinking (the topic of Borges's short story, 'Funes the Memorius').

To say this perhaps takes 'heritage' too much on its own terms. It is not interested in history, which it replaces with the notion of a timeless past which is still present (available in

11

present-day artefacts and souvenirs), but rather in present-day nationalism and tourism; the sites that get conserved – developed – are tourist venues, and what cannot become a matter for tourism is redeveloped. It exploits the 'heritage' it says it keeps, by being only interested in that heritage which will pay.[24] Its emphasis is unidirectional, requiring the visitor to read sites in a particular way. Going through the tunnel under the road to Stonehenge, you have no choice but to pass murals presenting fake images of Britain's past. Going to the Holocaust Museum in Washington, you are dispatched into an elevator by attendants who then shut the doors, as if sending you off to Auschwitz, leaving you to arrive alone on the top floor and to make the 'experience' by taking a compulsory direction down through the museum, so enforcing a particular preferred narrative and making return or re-reading difficult if not impossible. While it thus removes direct access, by museumifying, in making empathy compulsory, it *pretends* that direct access to other, historical experience is possible, as if there were no problem in co-opting the past into the present, as with the ideology that requires Shakespeare to be romped through regularly in the present-day live theatre, even with material such as *The Taming of the Shrew* or *The Merchant of Venice*. The results are often embarrassing. I put against direct access, the posthumous, by starting with the death of whatever text of the past it is that is being considered; but then also thinking that direct access is barred because of our own death.

While proposing the 'posthumous' in the face of other forms of the 'post', I want to avoid the *ressentiment* which would try to elevate the past above the present in importance (things were better then), and my starting point is that we *can* only begin with the present. Borges says that 'every writer *creates* his own precursors. His work modifies our conception of the past, as it will modify the future.'[25] The short story 'Pierre Menard: Author of the *Quixote*', where Pierre Menard rewrites fragments of Cervantes's text, to produce the same text but with meanings that have subtly shifted, concludes with the extension of this point about predecessors, by producing a new technique of reading that of the deliberate anachronism and the erroneous attribution. This technique . . . prompts us to go through the *Odyssey* as if it were posterior to the *Aeneid* and the book *Le jardin du Centaure* of Madame Henri Bachelier as if it were by Madame Henri Bachelier . . . to attribute the *Imitatio Christi* to Louis Ferdinand Céline or to James Joyce. (71)

The question here should not be 'why not' but how otherwise can texts be read, since these texts exist in the present. In opera productions, I agree with the American director Peter Sellars saying 'I hate updatings as a gambit. I resent it actively – it's cheap and vulgar and obnoxious and not to the point. My productions are never updated.'[26] Whether or not that is true of Sellars, updating seems to me a way of occluding historical difference, of denying the historical character of the piece. Peter Sellars's *Don Giovanni* (1987) set in contemporary Harlem, with an ethnically mixed cast of characters who seem to be drop-outs, purposefully chosen to be outside the range of sympathy of a contemporary opera audience, seems to me to be not an updating but to be more like Pierre Menard writing *Don Quixote*. The anamorphism of the text and music and the setting brings out irreconcilables that another, more mainstream production must cover over in the name of an imaginary continuity between the past and the present. This contrasts with the taste of those – the majority of opera-goers, probably – who like opera productions set in their time as costume-drama (*Don Giovanni* in 1787: an imaginary 1787, of course). But it seems over simple to attribute to the then *Don Giovanni* – or to any operatic text of the past – an ability to deal with all the material it handles; elements within the text did not cohere then, and remained as contradictions, while contradictions may now cohere, and elements that did not conflict may now appear as contradictions. To attempt to put the text back into the past attempts to assert that the past production had no troubling contradictoriness touching it, while updating tries to find equivalents for changes in historical time, as if denying historical difference. The same thing applies to productions of Shakespeare: in assuming that Shakespeare is performable today there is already an assumption that Shakespeare's plays worked in his own playhouse: an assumption which the present-day remake of the Globe theatre in London encourages by making theatre-going an enjoyment of and participation in a presumed 1590s experience.

Nonetheless, the past has been there, and may be thought as the posthumous. Barthes, perhaps thinking of the 'end of history', discusses the photograph as implying a flatness and completeness of representation, leaving the possibility that there is nothing else to say, which leaves open the question whether there is any future, any room left for anything new to appear: has saturation-point been reached? This is also Baudrillard's ground. But the photograph, which Barthes as a 'realist' – rather than as decoding those forms of realism which give the effect of the real – calls 'an image without code', is a record of death. It is a thanatography. Not just that it seems to strike the person imaged dead, in fixing them in a moment that will for ever seem unlike them, but in that, as Barthes says, it is 'not a "copy" of reality, but . . . an emanation of *past reality*' – which makes that reality posthumous, a form of living on in the photograph.[27] Photography disallows an evasion of the past, showing that reality cannot be constituted as an absolute, outside time; what is real belongs to a particular historical formation. Barthes makes the point that the century that invented history invented photography (93). Inventing history is an activity of modernity; the buildings and city-forms which were torn down by nineteenth-century bourgeois capitalists in the present are revived in simulacral form, as well as those newer industrial forms themselves in the century of the invention of tradition. Photography shows the present supplementing its reality by doubling it, and so keeping a perpetual present, comprising the present and something else as well, a posthumous present, enshrined in the photograph. The photograph then haunts the present with the thought of its posthumous being, as a record of a past.

5

The past is the posthumous. Musil thinks of his work in his life-time as posthumous; but we may also think of the present as the posthumous in relation to the past. Paul de Man, in 'Autobiography as De-facement', quotes Milton's poem on Shakespeare, 'What needs my Shakespeare for his honour'd Bones', affirming that Shakespeare needs no funerary monument. The poem addresses Shakespeare as if still alive:

> Dear son of memory, great heir of Fame,
> What needst thou such weak witness of thy name?

In turn this implies that the activity of reading Shakespeare, who is his own monument, his own funerary inscription, strikes the reader of the epitaph dead:

> For whilst to th'shame of slow-endeavouring art,
> Thy easie numbers flow, and that each heart
> Hath from the leaves of thy unvalu'd book
> Those Delphick lines with deep impression took,
> Then thou our fancy of itself bereaving,
> Dost make us marble with too much conceaving . . .

Paul de Man speaks of soulless bodies being left behind like statues, and adds that the line '"doth make us marble" . . . cannot fail to evoke the latent threat that inhabits prosopopopeia' (the literary device where the dead speaks, as if from a funeral inscription, saying 'Pause, Traveller', having been given a face and so a voice by the poem) 'namely, that by making the dumb speak, the symmetrical nature of the trope implies, by the same token, that the living are struck dumb, frozen in their own death'.[28]

To be made marble is to made mute, caught in the coldness of death. To be struck mute, brought into awareness of one's own death, is a powerful trope in Wordsworth, which Paul de Man explores through the example of the lines 'There was a Boy' from *The Prelude* (1805: V. 389–422). We can follow this trope, of the reader becoming posthumous, through two further examples.

In summer 1819 Keats wrote the opening to the fragment *The Fall of Hyperion*, which received posthumous publication. Keats

15

draws attention to the difference between the dreams of the fanatic and the poet. The first does not write his dreams, but the second does, and so secures a second life.

> For Poesy alone can tell her dreams,
> With the fine spell of words alone can save
> Imagination from the sable chain
> And dumb enchantment . . .
>
> Whether the dream now purposed to rehearse
> Be poet's or fanatic's will be known
> When this warm scribe my hand is in the grave.
>   (8–11, 16–18)

Spelling, written language, must replace the living voice with its 'enchantment'. The poetry will only be known as poetry when he is dead: it must become posthumous, because only then, when he is read as a figure from the past, will his distinction appear – whether as poet or fanatic. The posthumous writing will illuminate the poet. 'When this warm scribe my hand is in the grave' looks at the further change from handwriting to print; the appearance of a text in print means the death of handwriting. But handwriting cannot be seen as alive before it is translated into print. The hand will be in the grave when it has turned the words into handwriting. The activity of writing also makes both the subject, spoken of in the synedoche of the hand, and the subject-matter posthumous. The subject loses authority over utterance in the flow of textuality; the subject-matter becomes posthumous because the activity of writing turns that into the past.[29] The activity of reading in turn, turning the text into the past, further makes the reader posthumous.

Keats returns to 'the hand' in a posthumously published fragment of November 1819, one of his last written, and not a fragment in the sense that it needs anything else to complete its sense:

> This living hand, now warm and capable
> Of earnest grasping, would, if it were cold
> And in the icy silence of the tomb,
> So haunt thy days and chill thy dreaming nights
> That thou wouldst wish thine own heart dry of blood
> So in my veins red life might stream again,

And thou be conscience-calmed – see here it is –
I hold it towards you –

Within this poem, the living hand turns dead, 'see here it is': losing its name it is turned into a neuter pronoun, 'it'. The power of the neuter, the neither-nor, the not dead and not living, is Blanchot's theme; it is 'that which cannot be assigned to any genre whatsoever: the non-general, the non-generic, as well as the non-particular. It refuses to belong to the category of subject as much as it does to that of object.'[30] The neuter indicates a state in which the writer is rendered 'workless', or loses mastery, so that the hand which seems autonomous at the start, capable of earnest grasping, grasping the reader, has to be held out at the end. The present, the moment of writing, turns into the posthumous.

The hand is itself and it is also the poem, into which the hand turns, on the analogy of 'when this warm scribe my hand is in the grave'. The poem contemplates the act of becoming posthumous, through the act of writing (that is one sense of 'cold / And in the icy silence of the tomb') and – which may or may not be related – through the death of the author. Writing and the ghostly presence of the past would produce in the poem's reader not just the death-wish, but actual death – i.e. would produce wishing which had the force of killing, producing the reader of the poem as dead. The sixth and seventh lines read as both the expression of the wish (you would wish to desire so that red life might stream in my veins) and also as giving the result of the death – i.e. the death of the reader would produce the life of the text, 'and thou be conscience-calmed' – which could only happen by the death of the reader. In which case the last two lines could be read as the triumph over life of the hand: animated, it exists, as against the reader who is dead.

The poem implies an intricate allegorical relationship between the past and the present, or the present of the poem's writing and posterity. The power of the past, which includes what George Eliot calls in *Middlemarch* 'the dead hand', implies the power to grasp in the present through the power of representation, so that the power of the literary and the power of history go together. It is as if the poem, beginning with the conditional, 'would, if it were cold', asserts the possibility of such a power being exercised, through the writing of another poem, but the very possibility turns into a reality: 'see here it is – I hold it towards you –'. The possibility of a history and a posterity creates posterity as held by the past, already posthumous, but the fate of that posterity, whose existence puts the text into the past, depends also on the past being hollowed out, haunting and chilling. Thus the possibility announced in the second line, 'if it were cold', is not a possibility at all; the reader is already reading, and there is no alternative poem; the hand which is said to be warm and capable of earnest grasping is dead, in a posthumous state.

6

There is an affinity between this argument and the writings of Maurice Blanchot, for example the *récit* of 1948, *L'Arrêt du Mort* ('Death Sentence'), whose subject-matter is Paris in late 1938, after the Munich agreement with Hitler, and through to the fall of France in July and August, 1940. The title implies both the sentence prescribing death and the suspension of the enactment of death; it implies that point which Derrida in his commentary on the text calls 'living on', the state defined in Blanchot's *The Step Not Beyond*:

> To survive, not to live, or, not living, to maintain oneself, without life, in a state of pure supplement, movement of substitution for life, but rather to arrest dying, arrest that does not arrest, making it, on the contrary, *last. 'Speak on the edge – line of instability – of speech.'* As *if it attended the exhaustion of dying, as if the night, having started too early, at the earliest time of day, doubted it would ever become night.*[31]

Nothing that happens in *Death Sentence* relates to the public events of the history of the outbreak of the Second World War, though the text is intensely aware of those things, and bears the signs of trauma, in that the narrator says that he wrote a first version of the text, 'inactive, in a state of lethargy', in 1940, before destroying the manuscript (the word implies something written *by hand*). The narrator says 'I am talking about things which seem negligible, and I am ignoring public events' (162).

The things he writes about are not 'in the realm of things that can be told and experienced' (182) – they do not belong to a *roman,* which may be defined, in Blanchot's way, as 'the narration of an event' (447). The change in Blanchot from *roman* to *récit* is post-Auschwitz: it implies that there can now be no more narrating of a chain of happenings, an event which can be narrated and passed by; in the *récit* the narration *is* the event, 'an event which is yet to happen' (447), whose time has not yet passed, even though what has happened may, technically, be in the past.

J's death, which is the 'event' of the first half of the *récit,* is said to take place on Wednesday, 13 October 1938, which was actually a Thursday, so that her death is outside history, suspended, as if the events are made anamorphic to any history that can be told, and as if the effect of the *récit* is to abolish time, to de-realise history, neutralising it, giving it its death sentence. What is anamorphic is fragmentary, outside narrative (like the anamorphic skull in Holbein's painting *The Ambassadors*). It becomes the hole in the narrative, pulling everything towards it, including the public narrative. What remains is what is not narrative at all.

There are women in either half of the *récit,* J and Nathalie. Derrida, implicitly showing how the posthumous works, says that these are doubles, each the 'ghost, body at once living and dead, of the other. Separated: joined. There are two of them, absolutely different, absolutely *other* . . . But if the two women are different, utterly other . . . each one *is* the other. Each one signifies and preserves the other. Each sings the other's *arrêt de mort.* One dies *while* the other lives on, comes – again' ('Living On', 164–5).

In the first part of the narrative, the narrator has plaster casts made of J's hands; he says of them 'I cannot describe them, although at this very moment I have them under my eyes and they are alive' (137). It is hinted that these hands are what he calls 'the "living" proof of these events' but the word 'living' we can see is under erasure (for the casts are not living, not even 'living on'); and, in the next paragraph, he writes, 'because of something I did, someone had a very vague suspicion of this "proof" towards the end of 1940' (132), which means that the

19

word 'proof' is also under erasure. At the end, the other woman, Nathalie, says that she has had a cast made of her head and hands (and the narrator says, in a sentence he cannot complete, that this is 'a process which is strange when it is carried out on living people, sometimes dangerous, surprising, a process which . . .' (183)). She has it done, and he has somehow known it before. It seems to be the gift of (her) death; a gift which turns him, as the quotation shows, into speechlessness, as the *récit* is, as is said in 'The Song of the Sirens':

> the event itself, the approach to that event, the place where that event is made to happen – an event which is yet to come and through whose power of attraction the tale can hope to come into being too. (447)

The gift is that which takes away the power of narration, tipping him towards a posthumous state, a state of his own dispossession as the subject.

And death is where things start from, not from an originating subject:

> [T]his solitude has itself begun to speak, and I must in turn speak about this speaking solitude, not in derision, but because a greater solitude hovers above it, and above that solitude, another still greater, and each, taking the spoken word in order to smother it and silence it, instead echoes it to infinity, and infinity becomes its echo. (153)

Where speech is echolalia, its being is posthumous, and no more than the after-effects of something not accessible, as the past becomes the non-accessible, but there as a never-determinate thought, or obsession, whose identity can never be settled, 'and to that thought I say eternally "Come", and eternally it is there' (186). The words recall the end of the Book of Revelation, the Apocalypse, 'Come, Lord Jesus'.

At the end, in a passage which appeared in the first edition of 1948, was deleted in 1971 and then reappeared for the translation, the narrator says in words which also recall the curse on the reader of the Apocalypse who would take away or add to the words of the book:

> These pages can end here, and nothing that follows what I have just written will make me add anything to it or take anything away from

it. This remains, this will remain till the very end. Whoever would obliterate it from me, in exchange for that end which I am searching for in vain, would himself become the beginning of my own story, and he would be my victim. In darkness, he would see me: my word would be his silence, and he would think he was holding sway over the world, but that sovereignty would still be mine, his nothingness mine, and he too would know that there is no end for a man who wants to end alone.

This then should be impressed upon anyone who might read these pages thinking they are infused with the thought of unhappiness. And what is more, let him try to imagine the hand that is writing them: if he saw it, then perhaps reading would become a serious task for him. (187)

The narrator continues to add, in the act of saying that he is ending, by saying also that he is unable to end. The threat to the reader appears if the reader should obliterate 'it' – to do which would render the reader mute, making a new state of 'worklessness'. Texts 'live on' and a history which is not a history, not a *roman*, 'lives on' but without a determinate meaning (e.g. 'the thought of unhappiness'). The reader must further imagine the hand that is writing these pages; just as the writer has had the hands given to him in a process that gave him death while the hands' owner(s) were still alive. Imagining the hand that wrote would make reading 'a serious task', not allowing reading to be simply instrumental. It requires summoning up the past in a way which says that nothing of the past has finished. For 'not everything has yet happened' (152), either for a *roman* or for a *récit*.

That sense of being unable to find an *arrêt de mort* belongs to the anamorphosis that the text is: its replacement of a determinate history, its non-apocalyptic being. Steven Ungar speaks of the 'ghostlike quality of Blanchot's characters' and of a 'passivity' which he links to the 'posthistorical'.[32] Ungar compares that to the prevalence of the arguments of Kojève in 1930s Paris on the intellectuals who attended his lectures on Hegel. 'Post-histoire' means the end of the story of history: history as a narrative, history that can be told. It has come to an end in one of two ways, whose relation needs to be reflected on – either in Auschwitz, and what the death camps mean, or in the success story of the triumph of liberal American democracy. The 'living on' which follows would be what Walter Benjamin calls 'the catastrophe', but the catastrophic does not mean the end of everything, but rather the continuance of things as they are. One meaning of the apocalypse is continuation. Blanchot's *récit*, which also invites the apocalypse, in a different mode, and is apocalyptic, disturbs because of its relation to this 'post-histoire' – it is 'narrative' that can neither begin nor end, and its 'living on' is the power of the posthumous.[33]

7

I want to draw into discussion Derrida's essay 'Of an Apocalyptic Tone Recently Adopted in Philosophy', which has already been referred to. It makes several moves which may be summarised: (1) the apocalyptic tone is a form of exerting power; yet (2) the Book of Revelation reveals not the single truth-bearing Messianic logos, but gives place, rather, to the priority of writing and to 'dissemination' and to the irreducibly plural; (3) the apocalyptic is a form of dismantling power and the authority of the logocentric; and (4) as meaning the unveiling of truth, the sense of laying bare, it is the condition of all discourse, and if it is that, then the apocalyptic – except as it is already here – can never come; it is deferred, as much as it is promised within speech. The 'end of history' as an idea can be intimated but it is also subject to the power of *différance*, so there is always something else; the end must be for ever delayed.[34]

Derrida's essay, though it looks to no force to activate change, outside the conditions of discourse, works against the continuation of things as they are; it looks for that which will upturn the present course of things, whether or not they are at the end of history or 'post-histoire', as does Levinas, whose longing for change and a new ethical relation after Auschwitz makes him define language as 'the very power to break the continuity of being or of history'.[35] Blanchot's *récit*, by citing the apocalypse, looks for the event whose coming finishes the possibility of talking about a narrative of progress. I see such an event, following *Death Sentence*, as only possible on the basis of death, so that it belongs to the posthumous, just as 'end of history' arguments assign to the posthumous all elements of difference - all that does not fit with the homogeneity of global capitalism, presented as the narrative of the inevitable, incarnated in history as a history of progress.

The posthumous state, undecidable, like the apocalyptic, is outside history's patrilineal narrative. Julia Kristeva's work on abjection links the apocalyptic with the existence of taboos; for taboos customarily ward off the apocalyptic, keeping things in place, while the threat of the apocalypse transgresses taboos. Those taboos are what allows a history of progress, for they permit exclusions. In his essay, Derrida's linking of the Greek '*apocalupto*' – I uncover, I unveil – with the Hebrew '*gala*' enables a link with the idea that the apocalyptic reveals what has been hidden from narrative: 'enveloped, secluded, held back'. This means that the apocalyptic – especially if it is a condition of discourse – becomes a 'reincorporation of excluded contradictions',[36] which coincide not with the narrative of a history which has come to an end, but rather with the end of a certain history, which disallows otherness, the end of a history marked out by the idea of progress. It is that form of the apocalypse which is 'living on'.

8

Taking past and present as though they contained the possibility of the posthumous invites us to follow, as I do here, the posthumous as a trope. If past and present are caught up in the mutuality of the posthumous, is the past/present distinction workable? Which is living? Can we talk about texts of the past? Is it worth taking our present as posthumous, rather than as 'present'?

What follows in the next four parts addresses these questions through examples of the posthumous, beginning with it as an allegorical name, Posthumus, whose significance spreads till it touches every part of Shakespeare's play *Cymbeline*. The Latin 'postumus', which means 'last, late born' in sixteenth-century English, became 'posthumous' in spelling in order to create an etymology which would derive from 'humus', earth, or from 'humare', to bury: as if a change in spelling was needed to give the word dignity, or as if a word describing a condition which has no authority needed something extra. As newly spelled, it refers to what is after burial, after being laid in earth, and the *OED* gives 1591 for a first citation of the word in any spelling, barely twenty years before the time of *Cymbeline*. It belongs with the early modern period; it relates legally to the establishment of titles through patrilinearity. *Cymbeline*, which legitimates Britain as a nation-state through its creation of an imagined British history, also takes that away by making the posthumous an allegorical state and taking away that history.

In the second example, Dickens's David Copperfield says 'I was a posthumous child' because his father had died. Not to anticipate the second part, it should be noted that a posthumous child is not necessarily an orphan, and it would seem virtually impossible for 'the posthumous' to relate to the death of the mother before the birth of the child – so that 'the posthumous' relates to a lack within patriarchy, and an inability to be named, to receive the name of the father. The posthumous child, David Copperfield, who receives the impulse to narrate from that loss, is named for an absent father, which evokes his own lack of entitlement, so that he will be renamed constantly by others: Brooks of Sheffield; Daisy; Trotwood; Doady – names which include gender-changes. To be posthumous means losing the origin, so that the subject is established on the basis of an unknowable reserve, and it does not know what it is.

Calling a child 'posthumous' implies that it is dead; 'I was a posthumous child' implies both the state of being alive, surviving the father, but also, since it places death first, implying a state of death, so that the statement is as near as can be to the impossible statement 'I died'. The word 'posthumous' cannot be enlisted either on the side of life or death, and its undecidability allows thoughts of either other state to intrude on to the meaning that is being preferred. The word allows consideration of the presentness of the past (that it is dead) or the pastness of the present (that this is dead). To read texts of the posthumous is to reflect on this undecidability of meaning, and to see either state as allegorical of the other.

Autobiography asks who is the father; what is the David

Copperfield (DC)/Charles Dickens (CD) relationship? Does David Copperfield become metafictional by calling himself a posthumous child, denying a relationship to CD? In the 1867 Preface to the 'Charles Dickens Edition', the father says: 'I have in my heart of hearts a favourite child. And his name is DAVID COPPERFIELD', but this is the 'Charles Dickens', newly augmented by his edition, and he says it in *David Copperfield* so that it becomes a performative directing the reader how to take the text. The book authors the father.

The third part is also a 'personal history', Nietzsche's, in *Ecce Homo*. In this text, the father has never been there, and the text hardly produces him. He existed at the beginning of the child's life; but he does not take hold of Nietzsche because of the posthumous nature of being, its lack of a punctual connection with the present, which makes all being and all writing unauthored, unauthorised. The pressure that induces the trope of the posthumous comes from the person who does not wish to be situated in a determinate linear history which impels upon him the requirement to be this or something else. This text most fully of the four questions the cost of being free from the past.

The fourth example takes a trope of the posthumous in Walter Benjamin's 'Theses on the Philosophy of History' – written at the same crisis-moment as the events of Blanchot's *récit*, 'Death Sentence' – showing the past to be formed as history retroactively, from the standpoint of the present. Benjamin's need is to stop the logic of things going as they have up till now (sanctioned by a sense of history's uniformity) and to reclaim the past. Anything of history, therefore, solicits attention as the posthumous, as un-related to what has preceded it, having, and being, no father. Perhaps the posthumous suggests that only that state, as a char-acterisation of past and present, allows for living. In these four examples, the posthumous cannot have a determinate meaning, but it adds a third term to question the distinction between past and present, and to confuse a narrative based upon them.

Notes

1. Robert Musil, 'Art Anniversary', *Posthumous Papers of a Living Author,* trans. Peter Worstman (Harmondsworth: Penguin, 1995), pp. 79–80. This was his last completed work to appear in his lifetime. For Musil's relation to the posthumous, as it affects the novel he was working on from 1921 till his death in 1942, and parts of which appeared in 1930 and 1933, see the discussion by Burton Pike in Sophie Wilkins and Burton Pike's translation of *Der Mann ohne Eigenschaften – The Man Without Qualities,* 2 vols (London: Picador, 1995). It gives another sense of the 'posthumous' to think of this state beginning with his forced emigration from Vienna to Switzerland in 1938.

   A word on referencing: I have included first references to texts in notes, and after that have carried page numbers in the text. I have not bothered to give references where the source is obvious, or can be found in any standard edition; this is not that kind of scholarly book.

2. Maurice Blanchot, *The Step Not Beyond* translation of *Le Pas au-delà* by Lycette Nelson (Albany: State University of New York Press, 1992), p. 114.
3. See Sarah Kofman, *Smothered Words,* trans. Madeleine Dobie (Evanston: North Western University Press, 1998).
4. G. W. F. Hegel, *Aesthetics: Lectures on Fine Art,* trans. T. M. Knox (Oxford: Clarendon Press, 1975), vol. 1, pp. 11, 103.
5. Jacques Derrida, 'Of an Apocalyptic Tone Recently Adopted in Philosophy', *Oxford Literary Review* 6 (1984), 3–37.
6. Arthur C. Danto, 'The End of Art', in *The Philosophical Disenfranchisement of Art* (New York: Columbia University Press, 1986), p. 83.
7. Arthur C. Danto, *After the End of Art: Contemporary Art and the Pale of History* (Princeton, NJ: Princeton University Press, 1997), pp. 12, 113–14, see also p. 125. It will be seen that Danto's arguments allow for the return of the heterogeneous; in that sense they map on to the Derridean arguments about the apocalyptic suggested below.

8. Gianni Vattimo, *The End of Modernity: Nihilism and Hermeneutics in a Post-modern Culture*, trans. Jon R. Snyder (Oxford: Polity Press, 1988), p. 7.
9. Lutz Niethammer, with Dirk Van Laak, *Posthistoire: Has History Come to an End?*, trans. Patrick Camiller (London: Verso, 1992), pp. 57, 58. See Wolf Lepenies, *Melancholy and Society*, trans. Jeremy Gaines and Doris Jones (Cambridge, MA: Harvard University Press, 1992); pp. 177–97 give Lepenies on Gehlen. Lepenies's book appeared as *Melancholie und Gesellschaft* in 1969.
10. Quoted, Perry Anderson, 'The Ends of History', *A Zone of Engagement* (London: Verso, 1992), p. 343.
11. Kojève, in his influential lectures on Hegel in Paris, thought Hegel was right to see in the Battle of Jena (1806) 'the end of History', writing as a footnote to the second edition (1968):

> In and by this battle the vanguard of humanity virtually attained the limit and the aim, that is, the *end*, of Man's historical evolution. What has happened since then was but an extension in space of the universal revolutionary force actualized in France by Robespierre-Napoleon . . . the two world wars with their retinue of large and small revolutions had only the effect of bringing the backward civilizations of the peripheral provinces into line with the most advanced . . . European positions . . . the Sino-Soviet actualization of Robespierrian Bonapartism obliges post-Napoleonic Europe to speed up the elimination of the numerous more or less anachronistic sequels to its pre-revolutionary past. Already, however, this process of elimination is more advanced in the North American extensions of Europe than in Europe itself.

(Alexandre Kojève, *Introduction to the Reading of Hegel: Lectures on the Phenomenology of Spirit*, assembled by Raymond Queneau, ed. Allan Bloom, trans. James H. Nichols, jr (Ithaca: Cornell University Press, 1980), pp. 160–1.)
12. Jean Baudrillard, *America*, trans. Chris Turner (London: Verso, 1988), pp. 39, 30.
13. Gertrude Stein, *The Autobiography of Alice B. Toklas* (New York: Harcourt Brace and Co., 1933), p. 96.
14. James Joyce, *Ulysses*, ed. Hans Walter Gabler (London: Bodley Head, 1986), p. 28.
15. Jean-Philippe Mathy, *Extrême Occident: French Intellectuals*

and America (Chicago: University of Chicago Press, 1993), pp. 207–50.

16. For a summary, see '"End of Art" or "End of History"', in Fredric Jameson, *The Cultural Turn: Selected Writings on the Postmodern, 1983–1998* (London: Verso, 1998), pp. 73–92.

17. 'The word "history" has doubtless always been associated with the linear consecution of presence' – Derrida, *Positions*, trans. Alan Bass (London: Athlone Press, 1981), p. 56.

18. The imposition of narrative order is reactive (the product of Nietzschean *ressentiment*) – this is crucial to the argument of Sande Cohen, *Historical Culture: On the Recoding of an Academic Discipline* (Berkeley: University of California Press, 1986); this argues that 'historical thought' is 'a structure of defensive signification' and asks 'Can a nonreactive reader even read a historical text?' (p. 109).

19. Maurice Blanchot, *The Infinite Conversation*, trans. Susan Hanson (Minneapolis: University of Minnesota Press, 1993), p. 139.

20. Fredric Jameson, *Postmodernism: Or the Cultural Logic of Late Capitalism* (London: Verso, 1991), pp. 6, 25.

21. Walter Benjamin, *Understanding Brecht* (London: Verso, 1973), p. 121.

22. *Selected Prose of T. S. Eliot*, ed. Frank Kermode (London: Faber, 1975), pp. 38, 39.

23. Andreas Huyssen, *Twilight Memories: Marking Time in a Culture of Amnesia* (London: Routledge, 1995); p. 16 derives this point from Adorno.

24. See Barbara Kirschenblatt-Gimblett, *Destination Culture: Tourism, Museums and Heritage* (Berkeley: University of California Press, 1998). The interest in heritage culture may be marked by the publication of Eric Hobsbawm and Terence Ranger, *The Invention of Tradition* (Cambridge: Cambridge University Press, 1983).

25. Jorge Luis Borges, *Labyrinths*, ed. Donald A. Yates and James E. Irby (Harmondsworth: Penguin, 1970), p. 236.

26. Quoted, Jeremy Tambling (ed.), *A Night in at the Opera* (London: John Libbey, 1995), p. 69. The production is described in David Littlejohn, *The Ultimate Art* (Berkeley: University of California Press, 1992), pp. 130–55.

27. Roland Barthes, *Camera Lucida*, trans. Richard Howard (New York: Hill and Wang, 1981), p. 88.
28. Paul de Man, 'Autobiography as De-facement', *The Rhetoric of Romanticism* (New York: Columbia University Press, 1984), p. 78.
29. On this, see Timothy Bahti, 'Ambiguity and Indeterminacy: The Juncture', *Comparative Literature* 38 (1986), 209–23; Andrew Bennett, *Keats, Narrative and Audience: The Posthumous Life of Writing* (Cambridge: Cambridge University Press, 1994). Bennett derives his title from Joseph Severn watching Keats die: 'Each day he would look up in the doctor's face to discover how long he should live – he would say – "how long will this posthumous life of mine last" – that was more than we could ever bear – the extreme brightness of his eyes – with his poor pallid face – were not earthly' (quoted, p. 185). (The question also poses the other: who is it who refers to 'this posthumous life'?) Bennett's argument is that Keats's poetry must be read through a perception of his death throughout his writing.

Bennett's argument is obviously influential for this book: so is Massimo Cacciari's reading of modernism in Vienna, centring on Wittgenstein and circulating in the discourses of Nietzsche and Benjamin: *Posthumous People*, trans. Rodger Friedman (Stanford: Stanford University Press, 1996). Cacciari discusses a range of writers, including Musil, naming most of them on pp. 4–6, and says that his epigraph could have been taken from Wittgenstein, 'those who are merely ahead of their time deserve to have it catch up' (1). Posthumous people – the term derives from Nietzsche (see below, Part Three) – are not merely 'untimely, which implies the possibility of one day becoming timely (5); rather he quotes the Trieste-born writer Roberto Bazlen, that 'born dead, some succeed, little by little, in becoming alive' (173).

A third 'source' for my thinking about the posthumous is Hannah Arendt's Introduction to Benjamin in *Illuminations* (London: Jonathan Cape, 1970), pp. 1–51, when Arendt discusses him in terms of fame acquired during his lifetime and then posthumous fame – 'the lot of the unclassifiable ones . . . those whose work neither fits the existing order nor introduces a new genre that lends itself to future classification' (3).

30. Maurice Blanchot, *The Infinite Conversation*, trans. Susan Hanson (Minneapolis: University of Minnesota Press, 1993), p. 299.

31. Blanchot, *The Step Not Beyond*, trans. Lycette Nelson (Albany: State University of New York Press, 1992), p. 135. The translator notes for 'speak on the edge', 'speak on the arrête'. See Derrida, 'Living On: Border Lines', in Harold Bloom (ed.), *Deconstruction and Criticism*, p. 107. The text has been translated as *Death Sentence* by Lydia Davis; see *The Station Hill Blanchot Reader: Fiction and Literary Essays* (New York: Station Hill Press, 1999). This selection also contains 'The Song of the Sirens' (443–50), which discusses the distinction between a *roman* and *récit*.

32. Steven Ungar, *Scandal and Aftereffect: Blanchot and France Since 1930* (Minneapolis: University of Minnesota Press, 1995), p. 74.

33. 'Kojève had already said that the end of history was equivalent to the death of man. In all his works, Blanchot described this life after death which is the lot of man in the aftermath of history, and to which modern literature, in his view, is the supreme testimony' – Vincent Descombes, *Modern French Philosophy*, trans. L. Scott-Fox and J. M. Harding (Cambridge: Cambridge University Press, 1980), pp. 112–13. Blanchot followed Kojève in reading Hegel's work as a philosophy of death: death as that which is necessary for any development. See Leslie Hill, *Blanchot: Extreme Contemporary* (London: Routledge, 1997), pp. 104–7.

34. For these arguments, see Derrida's essay, pp. 23, 27–8, 29–30. David Wood, in *The Deconstruction of Time* (Atlantic Highlands, NJ: Humanities Press International Inc., 1989), pp. 378–83, takes issue with Derrida's contention that the apocalyptic is the condition of all discourse.

35. Emmanuel Levinas, *Totality and Infinity: An Essay on Exteriority*, trans. Alphonso Lingis (Pittsburgh: Duquesne University Press, 1969), p. 195.

36. This is the definition of the apocalyptic in Malcolm Bull, *Seeing Things Hidden: Apocalypse, Vision and Totality* (London:

Verso, 1999), p. 100. The Derrida discussion of 'gala' appears on pp. 4–5 of 'Of An Apocalyptic Tone . . .' Julia Kristeva's link of the apocalypse and the taboo appears in *Powers of Horror: An Essay on Abjection* (New York: Columbia University, 1981), p. 209.

Part One

Shakespeare's 'Opus Posthumous' – *Cymbeline*

1

*C*YMBELINE, PUBLISHED POSTHUMOUSLY, IN the Folio, was written some time after 1608. Walter Benjamin, taking the Baroque to figure the commodified modern state, where there is nowhere to go but for the culture to be folded in on itself and on its limits, says that 'the Renaissance explores the universe; the Baroque explores libraries. Its meditations are devoted to books.'[1] This makes *Cymbeline*, citing and re-staging earlier Shakespearian texts, Baroque. There is the jealousy of Othello (in Posthumus); Iago/Iachimo; and echoes of the rape of Lucrece; the Tudor invasion at Milford Haven in *Richard III*; the woman disguised as a boy from earlier comedies; the rings from *The Merchant of Venice*; the drug from *Romeo and Juliet*. Even names connect: in the Second Quarto for *Much Ado About Nothing*, Innogen was Leonato's wife as here she is wife of Posthumus Leonatus. And this Leonatus reappears, in another posthumous existence, as Leontes in *The Winter's Tale*.

In Holinshed, Cymbeline had reigned from 33 BCE, for thirty-five years, king of Britain when Christ was born:

Next him Tenantius raignd, then Kimbeline,
What time th'eternall Lord in fleshly slime
Enwombed was, from wretched Adams line
To purge away the guilt of sinfull crime . . .[2]

33

So Spenser in *The Faerie Queene* constructs a mythical national history. Shakespeare follows in another exploration of the library; but the significant event, the birth of Christ, takes place off-stage, in another jurisdiction (that of Augustus) and the play cannot refer to it. If it allegorises that event, it is undeclared. Is the play crafted to suggest that its events and its values are about to become out of time? The awkwardnesses of the plot, particularly its reconciliations, have often been commented on; but how does the sense of strain read: as something self-consciously artificial, preventing a sense that the final reconciliation can be taken as produced by natural growth?

One fear articulated in the play is of being excluded from history – as the young Arviragus, the son of Cymbeline, but brought up as a peasant and not knowing his destiny, feels when he says to his supposed father: 'What should we speak of / When we are old as you?' (III, iii, 35–6). The danger is to be untimely, marginal in relation to events which are elsewhere, having no more status than a parenthesis (the dominant trope in this play's language). Can there be a history in which the subject has part, or is the destiny of subjects to be no more than fragments of other events or scenes?

The play begins *in medias res*, and much of it is concerned with returning to a point of origin, which may be implied in the name 'Posthumus', in Holinshed, name of the posthumously-born son of Aeneas and Lavinia, grandfather of the Brutus who founded Britain. The name links Troy, Rome and Britain; while the play is silent on that, it is there to be picked up, to be integrated or not; another fragment. At the start, everything has happened irrevocably, as though we, coming into the play, are posthumous to its events – as, in *Hamlet*, the old king is posthumous to the play's opening by an imagined two months. Does the past then make the present posthumous? The First Gentleman gives the Second a historical narrative, hurrying on in a virtually uninterrupted speech. Cymbeline, the king of Britain has a daughter, Innogen, whom he wanted to marry to his new wife's son, Cloten. Innogen has, instead, married a 'poor but worthy gentleman', for which he has been banished. To the Second Gentleman's question, 'What's his name and birth?' there follows a genealogy of names whose history, larded with parentheses, locates the domestic antagonism at court in the context of Britain's resistance to Rome, the invading imperial power:

> I cannot delve him to the root: his father
> Was called Sicilius, who did join his honour
> Against the Romans with Cassibelan
> But had his titles by Tenantius, whom
> He served with glory and admired success:
> So gain'd the sur-addition Leonatus:
> And had (besides this gentleman in question)
> Two other sons, who in the wars o' th' time
> Died with their swords in hand. For which their father
> Then old and fond of issue, took such sorrow
> That he quit being; and his gentle lady,
> Big of this gentleman (our theme) deceas'd
> As he was born. The king he takes the babe
> To his protection, calls him Posthumus Leonatus,
> Breeds him, and makes him of his bed-chamber . . . (I, i, 28–42)[3]

Posthumus's father was called Sicilius; the name is Roman. But he has fought with Cassibelan against the Romans, the British king who it is said later (III, i, 5) paid tribute to Rome, and Cassibelan is not a Roman name. Roman imperialism produced British surrender. Sicilius received 'titles' from Tenantius, Roman name of another British king, presumably Cassibelan's brother and Cymbeline's father. Accordingly Sicilius received a Roman name: Leonatus, 'lion-born'.

Leonatus's two sons die in these colonial wars, and the father, 'doting on his children' (so J. C. Maxwell annotates 'fond of issue'), dies. He can see no future; his death self-excludes. It is said he 'quit being', as though in an abrupt cessation, implying something untimely, marking a history of failure, or imperfection. His wife too 'deceas'd' – the verb is active – at the birth of the youngest child. Cymbeline calls the baby Posthumus Leonatus, a name whose performativity attempts to define him as a continuation of his father; he is the hope for the continuation of what his father stood for. But in its superfluity, for why should anyone be given that name, except as if in mourning, and its character as a supplement to the sur-addition Leonatus – akin to the sur-addition Coriolanus, given to the hero who gains a title which he thinks puts him beyond the disempowering nature of the posthumous, since his dream is to be 'author of himself' (*Coriolanus*, V, iii, 36) – the name declares the child as lacking entitlement despite his father's 'titles'. Whereas the first 'sur-addition' meant a gain, an accretion, the second was a subtraction. 'Posthumus' announces a severance, a failure: the sons' deaths in the colonial wars has meant the father's death, and the allegorical inscription 'Posthumus' hangs over the court; as if the present time and regime both lack legitimacy.

The Gentleman gives other details apparently unrelated to this narrative. Cymbeline's two sons (Guiderius and Arviragus) were stolen in infancy so the king has only his daughter, Innogen, to succeed him. These missing sons, as figures of loss, evoke Posthumus's dead brothers. The court has become posthumous in character by their lack, so that Innogen's choice of Posthumus for a husband looks like a commitment to a nonlegitimated present, which is a reminder of past failure related to Britain as a colonised nation, and marked by failure, the sons dying with their swords in hand. While all in the court is said to be 'outward sorrow' – in contrast to the 'sorrow' of the old Leonatus – the king's anger at the marriage comes from him being 'touch'd at very heart' (I, i, 10), since the situation recalls a history of failure whose product in the present can only be melancholia.

Banished, Posthumus exists posthumously, beyond history: 'His fortunes all lie speechless, and his name / Is at last gasp' (I, vi, 52–3). *Cymbeline*, usually called a romance, along with *Pericles*, *The Winter's Tale* and *The Tempest*, may be taken as a tragedy (corresponding to its place in the Folio), or, considering its title, as a history. Can a history begin where present and subject are posthumous? Or is the play one of mourning? It contains mourning, hence the 'posthumous' spirit. The play is odd in genre-terms; the name and the word posthumous appearing only here in Shakespeare, but its very difference pulls Shakespeare towards the dominance of the posthumous as trope activating, or disempowering, all his work. While the play's romance spirit turns the posthumous towards a positive, unalienated state – possibly – this drive, towards unity and reconciliation, cannot silence other takes on posthumous being which link it with the untimely.

2

In Act 4, Innogen, disguised as a boy, Fidele, has come across her missing brothers in the Welsh mountains, not knowing their identity (they were stolen away from the court by Belarius). She has taken a drug, bringing about the appearance of death. The younger brother, not knowing her identity, lays the body on the stage, saying:

> With fairest flowers
> While summer lasts and I live here Fidele,
> I'll sweeten thy sad grave: thou shalt not lack
> The flower that's like thy face, pale primrose, nor
> The azur'd harebell, like thy veins, no nor
> The leaf of eglantine, whom not to slander
> Out-sweet'ned not thy breath: the ruddock would
> With charitable bill (O bill, sore shaming
> Those rich-left heirs, that let their fathers lie
> Without a monument!) bring thee all this;
> Yea, and furr'd moss besides, when flowers are none.
> To winter-ground thy corse. (IV, ii, 218–28)[4]

The parentheses in the quotation comment on a prevalent lack of mourning, indirectly evoking *Hamlet*, where mourning is always cut short. The speech is a form of mourning, as well as declaring its intention to remember, even if the other brother criticises its use of words – even, perhaps, finding their gender female – because, although it starts as what the brother will do for Fidele, it finishes as what the 'ruddock' (robin) will do; human agency disappears into the agency of nature, as if the text gives a premonition of human forgetting – the brother will only stay while summer lasts. The words are followed by another mourning, the dirge said by the two brothers:

> Fear no more the heat o' th' sun,
> Nor the furious winter's rages,
> Thou thy worldly task has done,
> Home art gone and ta'en thy wages.
> Golden lads and girls all must,
> As chimney-sweepers, come to dust.
>
> Fear no more the frown o' th' great,
> Thou art past the tyrant's stroke,
> Fear no more to clothe and eat,

To thee the reed is as the oak:
The sceptre, learing, physic, must
All follow this and come to dust.

Fear no more the lightning-flash.
Nor th'all-dreaded thunder-stone.
Fear not slander, censure rash.
Thou hast finish'd joy and moan.
All lovers young, all lovers must
Consign to thee and come to dust.

No exorciser harm thee!
Nor no witchcraft charm thee!
Ghost unlaid forbear thee!
Nothing ill come near thee!
Quiet consummation have,
And renowned be thy grave! (IV, ii, 258–81)

Speaking the dirge disallows consolations afforded by any form of decoration; the brother who had spoken of sweetening the grave with fairest flowers – like Gertrude throwing flowers on Ophelia's grave saying 'sweets to the sweet' (*Hamlet*, V, i, 236) – is not allowed such a supplement to grief; it is as though *Cymbeline* prefers what Hamlet calls 'maimed rites' (*Hamlet*, V, i, 213). After refusing the consolation of flowers, as an antithesis, the brothers say how 'golden lads and girls', flowers themselves, golden because they have taken their wages, which implies a completed life, must 'come to dust'. If death, like life, seems passive (Fear no more / Care no more), there are discoveries to be made within it, in the posthumous state, if only because to say these words implies a knowledge which is accrued from beyond death, so that death cannot be a firm border. When the dead person can be addressed, and it be hoped that he or she, now ghostly, will not be troubled by ghosts, death seems a truly equivocal state.

Resisting idealisation, the brothers *say* the words while recalling that at an earlier time they had *sung* them over their mother's body, Euriphile. The second occasion is a reminder of an earlier mourning, so that the present mourning accretes within it a mourning for that past occasion; mourning is both for the present loss for its recall of the past, and includes their own diminution of being: from singing their loss to saying it, as though their loss belonged to a general disenchantment of the world. Yet

Euriphile, the dead mother, Belarius's wife, was not their mother but their nurse.

When the dirge is said, two time-frames and several identities are interposed: burying the 'mother' and burying the fancied 'brother' as they call Fidele (III, vii, 44), who is actually their sister. It is part of the structure of the double image that neither time do the brothers bury the person they think they are burying. Perhaps all mourning is a representation which serves for the loss of something which, now being in the past, has a posthumous existence in what is now mourned. That would make mourning allegorical, as though what was being mourned was a displacement for something else. In this case it is concentrated on the mother, a displacement for another mother. As they have in the past sung a dirge to a mother, so Innogen, their sister, lying in the place of the woman who was a mother to the boys, virtually becomes her own mother. Later, posthumously revived, she becomes brother, sister, wife, mother, all at once.

One of the two brothers has just killed Cloten, who, dressed in Posthumus's clothes, wanted to kill Posthumus and to rape Innogen. The dirge finished, Belarius brings the headless body on stage, where it lies next to Innogen. The two bodies side by side, unburied and so lying in an unveiled, apocalyptic form, which arrests time and brings it to a standstill, make up an emblematic image; two people, one in death, one about to revive, one not. The image implies the posthumous, giving in one complex the dead and the beyond-dead.

3

Innogen has become a boy out of despair, since Posthumus, thinking that she is unfaithful to him, has commanded that she be killed. Becoming a boy is her way of escape. The Roman name she assumes as a boy, 'Fidele' – faithful – recalls her status as a wife, also evoking by contrast Posthumus, whom she calls 'false'. When she awakes she assumes the corpse next to her on the stage to be that of Posthumus, on account of the clothes it is wearing. Perhaps the same actor played Posthumus and Cloten, and the similarity runs close. Cloten was everything clottish and sexually violent and predatory: Posthumus has become suspicious of his wife, and would like to kill her. He has, as it were, lost his head, his reason, as Cloten has indeed lost his. Cloten in Posthumus's clothes allegorises what Posthumus is capable of becoming.

Innogen reviving is 'posthumous', having come out of a death where she has / has not 'died'. She took a draught that she thought was a restorative, but which her stepmother meant to be a poison. The doctor swapped the drugs, and it produced only the appearance of death. But since she has also been buried with funeral rites, and takes time to come to when she revives, it is as though she starts life again. Moreover, what she sees in this state is deceptive: the appearance is false, the body not her husband.

She sees a corpse which cannot revive, but in a sense it can. In Act II scene ii appears another image, also emblematic, that is, containing an allegory, which may be juxtaposed with this one. Innogen slept in her room, as though in another, earlier state of virtual death. She had allowed a trunk to be put in the room, because she associated the trunk with her husband – it contained, she was told, treasures he had collected. The trunk evokes her husband's body as a linguistic pun. Since the First Gentleman had already said of Posthumus 'I cannot delve him to the root', the husband's body is already being seen like a treetrunk, but the pun intensifies when a man climbs out of the trunk – Iachimo, whom her husband, Posthumus, had allowed to spy on her, to check on her faithfulness. When a man emerges from the trunk, that is another form of posthumous existence. When the man has taken what he wants (not her virginity – it may perhaps be assumed that Innogen and Posthumus have not slept together before he was banished by Cymbeline) he returns to the trunk. The posthumous revival is followed by another death.

Iachimo disappears into the trunk. Cloten, his head cut off, disappears into his own trunk, which is all that is left. Posthumus's being is signified by the trunk of the man lying on the stage, which Innogen sees when she wakes up. That trunk seems to embody both aspects of Iachimo and Cloten, as though both of these were part of Posthumus. At the end of the play, the man comes out of the dead trunk – Posthumus revived, driven to remorse and to a change of being after he believes that Innogen has been killed on his orders. In Georges Bataille's terms, he is *acéphale* – headless, no longer held by the impulse to dominate.

Innogen 'dies' as a boy, and wakes up alone as both disguised boy and wife as soon as she sees the dead body. Evoked as mother, brother and being really wife and sister, a golden lad and girl together, posthumous existence pluralises, or steps outside gender and gender relationships, making the character both male and female. At the end of the scene, the Roman Lucius finds her, and adopts her, calling himself 'father' (V, ii, 397). The only thing Innogen is not is the father; and of course, the word 'posthumous' assumes the father's death. When at the end of the play, she and her two brothers, now named as Guiderius and Arviragus, are reunited with their father Cymbeline, who is now twice a widower, he says, 'O what am I? A mother to the birth of three. Ne'er mother / Rejoic'd deliverance more' (V, v, 369–71). Deliverance is childbirth; it also creates posthumous identity: a mother, reversing Cymbeline's gender. The boys had sung a dirge for their mother, now they get another mother, as well as the brother they had also buried, now turned into a sister. Cymbeline's 'Oh what am I?' is a reflection on posthumous identity as double, and on the impact that the posthumous has on present identity. The dominant figure for the play is the posthumous; it embraces everybody: Posthumus, Innogen, Cymbeline, Iachimo, even Cloten, since his death allows for something posthumous, as implied in the sacrifice and ritual dismemberment he undergoes.[5] The posthumous permits Posthumus's revival of Posthumus in changed form.

When the posthumous becomes integral, involving resurrection before death in the case of Iachimo and his trunk, and being capable of repetition, it cuts out narrative order. The play becomes a series of mirroring tableaux, like the two images of the woman asleep and the 'trunk' next to her. To continue that theme would require noting that the narrative and narrative order accepted in the play – i.e. Innogen guilty, Innogen dead; the king's sons dead; Posthumus deceived into assuming his wife is guilty; Cymbeline deceived into thinking his present wife is innocent; Cloten planning to rape Innogen dressed as

Posthumus – must be replaced by another. Even the Soothsayer's interpretation of a dream (IV, ii, 346–52) turns out to be a misreading and must be replaced (V, v, 468–77). How the First Gentleman describes Posthumus in the first scene, in terms of his merits, is all part of a history which cannot stand, in view of Posthumus's later murderous intentions. And if narrative order depends on gender-order, both are destabilised by the posthumous.

4

Posthumus was the son of a Briton who fought against the Romans. His naming, however, is Roman; for Britain had submitted to the Romans, thus acquiring their names, and Cymbeline says of himself that (like a colonial subject about to rule in his own country) he was knighted by Caesar, and 'my youth I spent / Much under him; of him I gather'd honour' (III, i, 70, 71). Adopted by Caesar as patriarch, he has so adopted Posthumus, and named him. Exiled, Posthumus goes to Rome, returning to Britain with the Roman armies under Lucius, which have come to demand the tribute that Britain has lapsed in paying. Filled with remorse over the death of his wife at his demand, he disrobes himself of his Italian clothes to fight like a Briton peasant: 'so I'll fight against the part I come with' (V, i, 24–5).

The next scene (V, ii) shows the battle, which turns upon Belarius and Cymbeline's two sons joining in incognito, and reversing the Britons flying in retreat from the Romans down a narrow lane. Posthumus joins this 'stand' – a word repeated again and again (V, ii, 11, 13; V, iii, 1, 28,31) – and it leads to his account of the flight to one of the 'fliers' – i.e. the 'cowards' (the word appears three times) – beginning with how the Roman 'enemy' 'struck down' Britons:

> Some mortally, some slightly touch'd, some falling
> Merely through fear, that the strait pass was damn'd
> With dead men, hurt behind, and cowards living
> To die with lengthen'd shame.

And then how the word of the old man and the two young men affected the fliers:

> These three,
> Three thousand confident, in act as many, –
> For three performers are the file when all
> The rest do nothing, – with this word 'Stand, stand,'
> Accommodated by the place, more charming,
> With their own nobleness, which could have turned
> A distaff to a lance, gilded pale looks;
> Part shame, part spirit renew'd, that some, turn'd coward
> But by example (O, a sin in war,
> Damn'd in the first beginners) 'gan to look
> The way that they did, and to grin like lions
> Upon the pikes o' th' hunters. Then began
> A stop i' th' chaser; a retire: anon
> A rout, confusion thick: forthwith they fly
> Chickens, the way which they stoop'd eagles: slaves,
> The strides they victors made, and now our cowards
> Like fragments in hard voyages became
> The life o' th' need: having found the back-door open
> Of the unguarded hearts, heavens, how they wound!
> Some slain before, some dying, some their friends
> O'er-borne i' th' former wave, ten chas'd by one,
> Are now each one the slaughter-man of twenty . . .
> (V, iii, 10–13, 28–47)

Posthumus evokes a narrative reversal brought about from the men standing, and bringing things to a standstill. Britons were stabbed behind, now Romans are; the stand brings about 'a stop', a 'retire', and 'rout' – in a retrograde from Romans stooping as eagles to flying as chickens; from victors to slaves – while 'our cowards' become 'the life o' th' need', i.e. means of life in time of need, no longer mere fragments, but integral to life. The lane had been full of dead men, but 'some slain before' gain a posthumous existence, becoming, where ten had chased one, 'each one the slaughter-man of twenty'. Did the dead come to life? Has history been reversed? The historical account becomes an allegory, a riddle, an emblem, in a rhyme which Posthumus gives, omitting himself: 'Two boys, an old man twice a boy, a lane / Preserv'd the Britons, was the Romans' bane' (57, 58). It is the third memorialisation of this incident, which turns narrative history backwards by concentrating on a momentary image in which are held both possibilities, which makes it a riddle.

Posthumus then gives himself over to be arrested as a Roman. Imprisoned, he longs for death, and sleeps, and an apparition follows when there enters

> *Sicilius Leonatus, father to Posthumus, an old man, attired like a warrior, leading in his hand an ancient matron (his wife and mother to Posthumus) with music before them. Then, after other music, follow the two young Leonati (brothers to Posthumus) with wounds as they died in the war. They circle Posthumus round as he lies sleeping.*

The father accuses Jupiter of his treatment of Posthumus 'whose face I never saw / I died while in the womb he stay'd, attending Nature's law' (V, iv, 36, 37) while the mother, the 'gentle lady' of the First Gentleman's words, recalls that 'Lucina lent not me her aid, but took me in my throes / That from me was Posthumus ript, came crying 'mongst his foes / A thing of pity' (V, iv, 43–6).

The son, waking, says 'Sleep, thou hast been a grandsire, and begot a father to me . . .' (V, iv, 123–4). Sleep is described patriarchally, but that is to indicate that it can never be more than that ideal thing, a posthumous father-figure (for what is sleep if not a figure of death?). Sleep doubles the space of the present, making it so that a present generates the past. The past rises up in an image in response to an unstated need in the present, and Posthumus's vision is of the posthumous, since all those in it are dead. Produced by sleep in the present, the old man who appears can hardly be said to have been fathered; he has become real posthumously, through the nothing that is sleep. A child without a father is posthumous, and a child without parents an orphan, but Shakespeare's text grasps at the unnameable condition of a father who dies without seeing his son born, and a mother who dies before she gives birth. Or so the mother implies, altering the chronology of the First Gentleman, who said that she 'deceas'd / As he was born'. So he fails to 'delve [Posthumus] to his root'. The child is brought out of the dead mother (I do not think it is 'just' a caesarean birth that is being described), and the text recalls Macduff in *Macbeth*, who says, speaking about himself objectively, in the third person, as if making himself strange, that he was 'from his mother's womb / untimely ripped' (*Macbeth*, V, vii, 7, 15, 16).

'Ripped', a word whose violence implies the events of warfare, also evokes Posthumus as 'untimely'. Reading *Macbeth* in the light of the later play will allow the added interpretation that Macduff is also Posthumus, in relation not to a father, but to a mother.

The unnamed wife in the vision is 'ancient' as though she had gone on living after death. Walter Benjamin in 'The Storyteller' recalls the point that a man 'who died at thirty-five will appear *to remembrance* at every point in his life as a man who died at the age of thirty-five'.[6] Benjamin's context is the nineteenth-century novel, in which there is the implication that the 'meaning' of the character's life is revealed only in his death. That links the novel as a form to confessional statements; and not only to deathbed confession and deathbed statements, but more generally to the point that narrative closure is brought about in the closure of death, and constitutes the reader's authority with the sense that the characters in the novel have the status of confessants while he is the confessor. Benjamin writes, 'what draws the reader to the novel is the hope of warming his shivering life with a death he reads about' (101). Obviously, *David Copperfield*, one of whose draft titles was *The Copperfield Confessions*, has predominantly been read that way; the reader can feel a superiority to the characters of the novel. But it is not so with *Cymbeline*, where the absence of any glimpse of the mother as mother when she was alive means that she is revived in vision as old, as continuing in an afterlife. The untimely perpetuates its untimeliness in that the mother continues to grow old.

The old man and the two Leonati recall Belarius and his sons, all warriors against the Romans; they have been seen before, as so much of this play has been seen before in earlier plays. And returning to Act IV scene ii and to the dirge, it will be seen how its recall of the mother becomes proleptic for the revival in vision of *another* mother. One mother stands in for another. This is relevant in view of what Posthumus has said of her, at the point when he thinks that Innogen has betrayed him:

> Is there no way for men to be, but women
> Must be half-workers? We are all bastards,
> And that most venerable man which I
> Did call my father, was I know not where

When I was stamp'd. Some coiner with his tools
Made me a counterfeit: yet my mother seemed
The Dian of that time: so doth my wife
The nonpareil of this. (II, iv, 153–60)

The hysteria of this turning against the mother leads to the will to 'find out / The woman's part in me' (II, iv, 171–2), in a sentence which receives no ending. Made a 'counterfeit' by some coiner with his tools, which may mean that he is not truly posthumous (his father may be alive; Posthumus may be a counterfeit with regard to his name), he is also a counterfeit man, so that he writes to Pisanio as though he was a violated woman: 'thy mistress, Pisanio, hath play'd the strumpet in my bed; the testimonies whereof lies bleeding in me' (III, iv, 21–3). To become posthumous would give freedom from such anxiety of identity or gender, and it is significantly a need the male feels. The 'woman's part' in the male would include the singing voice.[7] This is what the young men who say the dirge lack; their mourning is for the loss of the woman's part, as is complexly true when they bury Fidele. For they bury the woman thinking it is a man; they rebury their mother; they bury the wife that Posthumus would like to have seen killed; they memorialise their own former voices from the standpoint of their 'mannish crack' (IV, ii, 236), and while they are conscious that they should not 'play in wench-like words' (IV, ii, 230), the constraint upon their mourning makes it as if male mourning – unconsciously – is men mourning that they are not women. When Posthumus fights against the part he comes with (V, i, 24, 25), the logic implies that since he comes as a (Roman) male, who has been intent on wife-murder, now the woman's part in him (which also makes him a Briton peasant) fights the man's part. This restages colonial resistance in gender terms. The Briton peasant garb – which aligns him with Innogen's male costume – as it were feminises him (so that the whole narrative of the resistance to the Romans in pursuit involves a gender shift: the three effect such a change like turning 'a distaff to a lance').

The dirge spoken to the boy who is really the woman who was so slandered that it led to Posthumus slandering his dead mother contains in itself an answer to that original injustice, embodied in 'Fear not slander, censure rash'. The apparition of the mother

46

in Act 5 shows the persistence of 'the woman's part', which in some way is born out of the death-like dream of Posthumous. Recalling the past means imagining it in relation to the woman's loss. When Innogen dressed as a boy, Pisanio said, 'You must forget to be a woman' (III, iv, 156), but the mother's words and appearance reverse that reading of history, a reminder that the feminine is at the heart of the engendering of both memory in that act of mourning and of the effort to work with the fragmentary – as Benjamin puts it, 'mourning is at once the mother of the allegories and their content' (*The Origin of German Tragic Drama*, 230).

5

The symmetry in the apocalyptic moment of those two bodies, one torso, one whole, lying on stage in a silent space of time fits with an image whose implications are tilted towards the neatness of a reconciliatory symbolism, the direction the play proceeds in, however artificially. Considering the play in its afterlife, however, 400 years on, can its movement towards reconciliation be accepted so easily, even if the situation is accounted as like medieval allegory in its lack of realism? Does not that by de-realising the situation, also threaten to trivialise it? A headless body – how would that relate to Levinas discussing the priority of the face of the other in terms of my relation to that other? ('The way in which the other presents himself, exceeding the idea of the other in me, we here name face'.[8]) Do we discard the point in a present reading, as not relevant? But we cannot quite forget it, even so. Does not the play risk making its symmetries replace another awareness: that of the broken, fragmented and out of time, moving instead towards a near fluent desire to reconcile everything, to exist in a completeness of fulfilment that would be absolute?

6

Macduff's words that he was 'from his mother's womb / Untimely ripped' link with Walter Benjamin on Baroque allegory.

> Whereas in the symbol destruction is idealized and the transfigured face of nature is fleetingly revealed in the light of redemption, in allegory the observer is confronted with the *facies hippocratica* of history as a petrified, primordial landscape. Everything about history that, from the very beginning, has been untimely (*Unzeitiges*), sorrowful, unsuccessful, in expressed in a face – or rather, a death's head.[9]

The Romantics, such as Goethe, or Coleridge, validated the symbol as a form of integrating human experience with nature, with the natural. The organic growth of symbolism points to the triumph of natural order within time. To that, Benjamin opposes allegory, the form reached towards by the melancholic, who is perhaps in the realm of 'post-histoire' – and who cannot believe in structure, which would belong to nature and to history. In allegory, 'nature' is replaced by history; and, in contrast to a history of 'progress', where the past is fulfilled in the present, Benjamin's 'untimely' relates to history as unfulfilled, the place of lost time, having no coincidence between an event and anything that can be made of it to give it a meaning. That is the danger faced throughout *Cymbeline*. Writing in the symbolic mode implies one attitude to history – which sees it in terms of natural growth – but the allegorical mode implies another. The tendency of the symbolic is towards the face of nature as benign; allegory looks at history, in movement, change, putting its own writing against that which has no essential being. It uses the death's head as an image, for this implies going below the surface appearance. Benjamin speaks of the 'majesty of the allegorical intention: destruction of the organic and living – the extinguishing of appearance'.[10] No idealisation is possible when 'the key figure of the early allegory is the corpse' (55). The 'organic and living' imply representations of history as natural, where the present has constructed the past as living tradition, continuous into the present which it feeds, as organic, single and developmental, existing in a chronological narrative. Where no natural meanings can be sustained, history appears as a petrified, primordial landscape.

Though the posthumous aligns with the untimely, *Cymbeline* moves – if ambiguously – towards the symbolic mode: natural harmony, clarification of riddles and doublenesses of meaning, as if it is hard to resist the consolations that seem to offer full presence and meaning, as the symbol does. At the beginning, the First Gentleman says: 'You do not meet a man but frowns: Our bloods / No more obey the heavens than our courtiers / Still seem as does the king's'. This can be glossed in different ways. Our temperaments follow planetary influences to the same extent that our courtiers, by frowning, which is their 'seeming', their pretence, follow the king. But our bloods (passions) do *not* obey the heavens (i.e. religious virtue), even if our courtiers do seem to follow the king, who, in this case, is clearly wrong – so that the alignment of king / heavens is odd, and the frowning double. Are the courtiers frowning because they follow the king's lead, or because they dislike being told what to do (as passions cannot obey the dictates of virtue)? If the courtiers represent the heavens, their 'frowning' – like an angry sky – makes others ('our bloods', the Gentleman is speaking for himself) discontented. Are the courtiers frowning in reality or not? Perhaps it comes to the same thing; hence, 'Fear no more the frown o' th' great.' 'All is outward sorrow' it seems, but:

> not a courtier,
> Although they wear their faces to the bent
> Of the king's looks, hath a heart that is not
> Glad at the thing they scowl at. (I, i, 12–15)

The double negative, the antitheses of face and heart, glad and scowl, twists or bends sense so that it is not clear which emotion dominates; and in any case, how would the First Gentleman, whose overpraise of Posthumus appears next, know? What would be the marker of the difference between the two emotions?

The first scene, like the unreadable torso that Innogen wakes besides, suggests the ambiguity of appearance which is basic to allegory and what it works on, and the impossibility of moving from appearance to anything more real. Frowning and scowling and outward sorrow are signs of a melancholic discontent where there is a basic unfitness, like that between the bloods and the heavens, making whatever happens on the surface unreliable. This could be developed further. The dirge says 'Fear no more the lightning-flash, Nor th'all-dreaded thunder-stone' as if pointing to the peremptory nature of power. In V, iv, after the apparitions' complaint to Jupiter, he '*descends in thunder and lightning, sitting upon an eagle: he throws a thunderbolt. The Ghosts fall upon their knees.*' The 'all-dreaded thunder-stone' imposes an order whose absolutist form makes the words of the dirge proleptic, save that death does *not* finish the threat of the thunderbolt. The Ghosts' effusive submission to Jupiter becomes analogous to the way our bloods obey the heavens; for the plaint is not replied to by Jupiter in a way that takes up past history. The outward obedience of the ghosts need not be distinguished from appearance only.

What clarifications take place in the last scene, taking away ambiguity, may be seen as the imposition of a law which is inseparable from the symbolic idealisation and commitment to the surface. As *Cymbeline* moves towards closure, towards symbol and from allegory, its politics and history thin out, into a reconciliation between Rome and Britain, expressed in the victorious British agreeing to pay tribute to the Romans. Was that the answer to the past wars? At that point, identities are settled and the comparative loss of ambiguity means a settling for appearances: things at the end are what they seem to be.

7

The question of history is raised in *Cymbeline* by reference to the ghosts that appear to Posthumus. Imprisoned, Posthumus mourns on account of Innogen whom he believes dead, and is melancholic because of his self-hatred; recalling Freud's distinction that 'in mourning it is the world which has become poor and empty; in melancholia it is the ego itself'.[11] Perhaps Posthumus has always been a melancholic; that, relating to his name, would account for something in Freud's description of melancholia that otherwise would not fit:

> profoundly painful dejection, cessation of interest in the outside
> world, loss of the capacity to love, inhibition of all activity and a
> lowering of the self-regarding feelings . . . that finds utterance in
> self-reproaches and self-revilings, and culminates in a delusional
> expectation of punishment. (252)

This melancholia appears in the desire not to show emotion (I,
ii, 23–6), in his inability to fight Cloten (I, ii, 92–4), and his readi-
ness to test Innogen, and the failure of his rage to become
anything as he closes the speech in which he attacks and abuses
the absent Innogen for deceiving him (II, iv, 183–6). Indeed, in
that speech of fury, the assumption of a more powerful lust in
his rival than he possesses himself ('a full acorn'd boar, a German
one, / Cried "O" and mounted' [II, iv, 168–9]), appears a melancholia which it may be surmised belongs personally to a failure
to mourn his dead parents, to embrace his name's meaning. And
again, this would link with Hamlet. Such a melancholia has
perhaps been working in all from the beginning of the play ('You
do not meet a man but frowns'),[12] and it has to do with the past
being posthumous, the present being also dead. It is not
surprising that Posthumus has failed to kill Cloten in a duel,
since – against all logic – 'he had no help of anger' (I, ii, 93);[13]
nor that he should be so obsessed with cowardice on the field,
tracing that back, in an odd phrase, which recalls this play's obsession with origins, to 'first beginners'. Imprisoned, he asks the
gods for death:

> For Innogen's dear life take mine, and though
> 'Tis not so dear, yet 'tis a life; you coin'd it . . . (V, iv, 22–3)

He returns to the language of coining that he has used before
(II, iv, 156–8) from which I have already quoted. Returning to
this, it becomes apparent that the name 'Posthumus' cannot be
the name of a complete state. The character is not posthumous
because the father who is Jupiter 'coins' life. Posthumus is still
fathered; what is positively posthumous in him relates more to
the mother, if she indeed died before he was born. In the same
way, Innogen, who preserves a memory of her mother (I, ii, 43,
III, iv, 2, 3) while her oppressive father is alive, approaches that
same condition.

The theme of the apparitions is Jupiter's 'spite' against

Posthumus (V, iv, 31). But this raises questions. When Innogen sees the headless body of Cloten, in an act of prosopopeia she refers to 'his Jovial face' (IV, ii, 311) – just as Hamlet said of his father that he had 'the front of Jove himself' (*Hamlet*, III, iv, 56). No doubt the trope is common. But Innogen unconsciously makes her dead husband the patriarch; in a comparison with *Hamlet*, it will be remembered that Hamlet was not posthumous, for the First Clown records that he began grave-digging – recording the presence of death – 'the day that our last king Hamlet overcame Fortinbras . . . it was that very day that young Hamlet was born – he that is mad and sent into England' (*Hamlet*, V, i, 144–8). The old king's show of violence as it were confers death and madness on his successor; there is an imperial history there which spites the present, and it is what the posthumous person evades. But in a way, *Hamlet* is a posthumous play for 'those who are mutes and audience to this act' (V, ii, 335) since it is begun after the old king is dead; struck dumb, able only to hear, as though ghostly. Hamlet's own paralysis is because he is and is not posthumous; if Posthumus were alive when Innogen spoke, he would have the face of the patriarch who is not the right choice of god for those fighting against the Romans.

Hence, these unlaid ghosts, whose resistance to the Romans is emphasised in the Second Brother speaking of dying for 'our country's cause' and of their loyalty to Tenantius (V, iv, 71–4), pray to the wrong god: Jupiter, the Roman, imperial god who appears with the Roman eagle. In the dirge came the prayer 'No exorciser harm thee', as though the worst thing that could happen to a ghost was to be raised, like the spirit of Samuel to Saul (I Samuel 28: 15: 'Why hast thou disquieted me to bring me up?'). These ghosts have not escaped from history in their deaths, but are forced to appeal to a system which has been unjust to them, to pray in that language which is oppressive, which links with a different history in which they have no part. They are already, necessarily, figures of a postcolonial *ressentiment*; and if it is true that 'the dead hate the living', as Fredric Jameson argues about ghosts in discussing *Spectres of Marx*, in part of his argument that 'there is no "proper" way of relating to the dead and to the past',[14] they are already ambivalent, both towards the god they pray to and the living man they defend.

Their appearance as part of Posthumus's dream dramatises the other aspect of his melancholia. Freud writes that 'the woman who loudly pities her husband for being tied to such an incapable wife as herself is really accusing her *husband*' which leads him towards the aphorism that 'complaints are really "plaints" in the old sense of the word' – or, as Nietzsche puts it, for Freud took it from him, 'all complaining is accusation' – 'Alles Klagen ist Anklagen' (*The Wanderer and his Shadow*, section 78). In prayer, Posthumus *justifies* the gods. In his dream he *accuses* them through the fantasised form of his parents and his brothers, in speeches that justify him, allowing no shadow of blame to fall upon him.

The ghosts ventriloquise Posthumus's anger, which is directed against patriarchy, where that takes three forms: (1) Cymbeline's injustice; (2) the Romans as figures of domination, even giving the Britons their names; (3) the Roman gods. While the ghosts justify Jupiter after he has descended on his eagle, that servility may be read as a continued accusation. The passage raises the issue of the relation of perceptions of injustice to *ressentiment*, and the claim of past injustice, past loss and past failed potential to speak in the present, though the ghosts' *ressentiment* about the past means that when they speak for Posthumus, they idealise him. Failure in grasping what has happened in the past implies failure in grasping the present, and the history here is different from the triumphalist narrative implicit in *Cymbeline* as related to *The Fairie Queen*.

The dream comes from two sources. First from the present melancholia of Posthumus, where the dream is like writing that the melancholic produces as a supplement to validate the ego. This melancholia extends to his construction of a past history; but as dream, it embodies the perpetual unappeased state of the past. Instead of haunting the living, as in *Hamlet*, which is the direction to which ghostly hatred might be expected to turn, the ghosts turn against patriarchy.

This has three results. Patriarchy is massively re-asserted through the vision of Jupiter, which makes talk of the 'posthumous', in regard to patriarchy, impossible. To become posthumous, then, would be the expression of a *desire*. It means being free of Jupiter, being unlike a 'poor wretch, that depend[s] / On greatness' favour', and who after dreaming (hoping for something) 'wake[s] and find[s] nothing' (V, iv, 127–9). The words of Jupiter produce a new servile obedience of the spirits, which seems itself to justify patriarchy. The third effect is the 'tablet' Posthumus finds laid across his breast, which he cannot understand, but which makes him say 'the action of my life is like it' (V, iv, 15), as though making his life an allegory. It is as if when he wakes he finds an epitaph upon him (as if marking him as beyond the tomb, posthumous again) – unlike Innogen, whose grave was unmarked, or Timon of Athens who fashions his own epitaph. The writing is reconciliatory, but, in contradiction of this, Posthumus comes under the power of the superscript written by patriarchy.

His waking existence continues his dream existence, which parallels Innogen, whose waking from her drugged sleep and with no epitaph above her begins by recalling her life as Fidele, thinking of it as a dream, and adding:

> The dream's here still: even when I wake, it is
> Without me, as within me: not imagin'd, felt. (IV, ii, 306–7)

Seeing her continued existence as a dream makes it double: not either/or, but both/and. She does not go fully outside the dream, which becomes like the posthumous state denied to Posthumus, not ghosted by the writing which haunts Posthumus's existence, with loss of subjectivity and existence being directed from without, or like the allegorical writing which seems to ghost Posthumus's existence.

Being posthumous in this way means to become part of a celebratory history, which is what the play turns to in the final scene. Though the epitaphic riddle is incomprehensible, its destiny is to be explained in single terms – as the rhyme he gives to the 'flier' is not explained, but left ambivalent – when patriarchy visibly takes control again. This happens in the union of Cymbeline with the Roman Lucius and in the re-instatement of a royal lineage. It seems as if a 'posthumous' state, like an unmarked grave, cannot be allowed existence: hence the contradiction which is implied in the lines 'Quiet consummation have / And renowned be thy grave'. The symbol, and the desire for interpretation, and for a 'natural' fulness, takes control. A history whose tragedy produces the notion of the 'posthumous' is always in danger of being reclaimed for a beneficent patriarchal force so that there are more fathers at the end of the play than at the beginning. (Jupiter's words that Posthumus was married in his temple might be considered an exclusion of the woman's part – in this context, Juno, goddess of marriage.)

Nonetheless, the challenge from Posthumus's dead mother, who was also a victim of the colonial wars, if only indirectly, is not so easy to assimilate. Posthumus's hatred of the 'woman's part' commits him to patriarchy, even if that is a position he later resists. But the *mother's* death as that which makes Posthumus posthumous implies the ending of a belief in an originary nature, which could be revealed in the neatness of symbolism, and the commitment to seeing that there is nothing other than history, which is what Benjamin's allegory works with. In *Paradise Lost*, the archangel Michael tells Adam to live temperately, 'till like ripe Fruit thou drop / Into thy Mother's lap' (*Paradise Lost*, XI, 535–6); but that perception of death and of nature as the mother, which is the basis of Freud's essay on the 'Three Caskets', is not available to the person whose mother dying before his birth allegorises the loss of an enclosing originary nature, so making it apparent that there can be no 'natural' solution or resolution to any historical crisis.

The dead mother's words, referring to Lucina, the Roman goddess who did not aid her, imply further the impossibility of thinking in terms of nature in relation to transfiguration, or thinking that there can be anything which can be called 'natural'. If there is nothing else save history's untimeliness, then the posthumous state is that which is cut off from any pre-given right order, or any 'correct' meanings. In Baroque allegory, Benjamin says,

> [A]ny person, any object, any relationship can mean absolutely anything else. With this possibility a destructive but just verdict is passed on the profane world: it is characterised as a world in which the detail is of no great importance. (175)

Hence, as Benjamin said, the Renaissance looked outward, but the Baroque looks inward to the library, to fragments of knowledge, to old knowledge. If these are revived, it is with the sense that there is no true time in the world in which they can find their existence.

Where things are untimely and unsuccessful, details disappear, but Benjamin's commitment to a non-repressed history runs against that when the 'Theses on the Philosophy of History' contend that 'only a redeemed mankind receives the fullness of its past – which is to say, only for a redeemed humanity has its past become citable in all its moments' (*Illuminations*, 256). *Cymbeline* finishes with the publication of 'peace' (a word resounding through the last few speeches, from the Soothsayer's words onwards), which sends the actors out of the London theatre, and implicitly, into a triumphal march through 'Lud's town'. The play symbolises national revival, and constructs a national history, but the allegorical details that are not fully 'citable' at the end indicate that much must be left behind. The strained interpretations of the 'tender air' and the 'lion's whelp' and the 'lofty cedar' and the flight of the lofty eagle, while they seem to have symbolic force and therefore to fit the celebratory Romance ending, lean rather to allegory (since the meaning is 'so from sense in hardness' (V, v, 432), where 'sense' means both 'meaning' and 'nature') and to the point that there can be no 'natural' interpretation. Similarly, the arbitrary nature of the history that is to be constructed – joining forces with Rome – threatens the sense of a natural ending, and leaves the questions about history deliberately unanswered. All fails to resolve itself into the symbolic mode. Historically, neither in performance nor in study has the play satisfied those who look for a perfect Romance ending, and in that way it leaves room for thinking that its most interesting things are part of another, buried history, which casts its characters as posthumous, while the dominant history continues without them. The dirge, deliberately anachronistic to evoke the period of the absence of consolation before Christianity, will become implicitly out of date with the introduction of the Christian narrative with which it implicitly contrasts; as though the writer had deliberately evoked a dead period. If the dirge remains the most famous part of the play, that commitment is also on the side of the allegorical, not the symbolic, drive of the play. The play's drive towards a symbolic state shows its kinship with triumphalism, with the desire to expunge the posthumous as the other in the name of creating a consistent history which has its own telos in the eagle – now female and so now the more 'natural' (V, v, 471–7) – flying into, and losing herself in the west. And why should she stop at Britain when Shakespeare's own Britain had its own triumphalist sense of the golden west?

Notes

1. Walter Benjamin, *The Origin of German Tragic Drama*, trans. John Osborne (London: Verso, 1977), p. 140.

2. Spenser, *The Fairie Queene*, Book 2, canto 10, stanza 50. On this topic, see the essays by Philip Brockbank, 'History and Histrionics in *Cymbeline*' and Emrys Jones, 'Stuart *Cymbeline*', both in D. J. Palmer (ed.), *Shakespeare's Later Comedies* (Harmondsworth: Penguin, 1971). Both are dependent on G. Wilson Knight, *The Crown of Life* (1947; London: Methuen, 1965), pp. 129–202. A more critical sense of the play appeared in F. R. Leavis, 'The Criticism of Shakespeare's Late Plays', *The Common Pursuit* (Harmondsworth: Penguin, 1962), pp. 173–81. A recent reading of the play in relation to a national history appears in Leah Marcus, '*Cymbeline* and the Unease of Topicality', in Kiernan Ryan (ed.), *Shakespeare: The Last Plays* (London: Longman, 1999), pp. 134–68; another in Jodi Mikalachki, *The Legacy of Boadicea: Gender and Nation in Early Modern Britain* (London: Routledge, 1998), pp. 96–114. For the play and psychoanalysis, see Meredith Skura, 'Interpreting Posthumus's Dream from Above and Below: Families, Pyschoanalysis and Literary Critics', in Murray M. Schwartz and Coppelia Kahn (eds.), *Representing Shakespeare* (Baltimore: Johns Hopkins University Press, 1980), pp. 203–16, and Ruth Nevo, *Shakespeare's Other Language* (London: Methuen, 1987), pp. 62–94. See also Heather Dubow, *Shakespeare and Domestic Loss: Forms of Deprivation, Meaning and Recuperation* (Cambridge: Cambridge University Press, 1999), pp. 120–41.

3. Quotations from *Cymbeline* from Arden edition, ed. J. M. Nosworthy (1955; London: Thomas Nelson, 1997); other

editions of *Cymbeline* consulted are the New Cambridge (ed. J. C. Maxwell, 1960) and the Oxford (ed. Roger Warren, 1998). I have followed the Oxford edition in calling the heroine 'Innogen' (innocent), rather than the more conventional 'Imogen'. Other Shakespeare references use the Riverside Shakespeare, ed. G. Blakemore Evans (Boston: Houghton Mifflin, 1974).

4. I have not accepted the Arden punctuation here which makes the speech unfinished: see the readings by Maxwell and Warren.
5. That he is to become a sacrifice is hinted at in I, iii, 2.
6. Walter Benjamin, 'The Storyteller', *Illuminations*, p. 100.
7. I take this point from *Twelfth Night*: Orsino to Viola disguised as Cesario: 'thy small pipe / Is as the maiden's organ, shrill and sound, / And all is semblative a woman's part' (I, iii, 32–4).
8. Emmanuel Levinas, *Totality and Infinity*, p. 50. I have dropped Levinas's emphases.
9. Walter Benjamin, *The Origin of German Tragic Drama*, p. 166.
10. Walter Benjamin, 'Central Park', *New Left Review*, 34 (1985), p. 41.
11. Freud, 'Mourning and Melancholia', *The Penguin Freud*, 11 (Harmondsworth: Penguin, 1977), p. 254.
12. Compare the speech on melancholy in IV, ii, 203–8.
13. Note the contrast with Coriolanus; compare the spirit of I, ii, 97–100 with *Coriolanus*, IV, ii, 23–5. Innogen is more aggressive.
14. 'Marx's Purloined Letter', in Michael Sprinker (ed.), *Ghostly Demarcations: A Symposium on Jacques Derrida's Spectres of Marx* (London: Verso, 1999), pp. 39, 57–8.

Part Two

Without Origins: *David Copperfield*

I was a posthumous child. My father's eyes had closed upon the light
of the world six months, when mine opened on it. There is something strange to me, even now, in the reflection that he never saw
me, and something stranger yet in the shadowy remembrance that
I have of my first childish associations with his white grave-stone in
the churchyard, and of the indefinable compassion I used to feel
for it lying out alone there in the dark night, when our little parlour
was warm and bright with fire and candle, and the doors of our
house were – almost cruelly, it seemed to me sometimes – bolted
and locked against it.[1]

1

DAVID COPPERFIELD OCCUPIES A position more centre-stage
than Posthumus, since he is not a colonial subject, but
relates to Britain at the time of its colonial expansion. Hence
so much of an apparent confidence within *David Copperfield*. The
hero seems so confident of his powers of knowledge, or so interested in playing the detective, that he calls the first chapter, 'I
am born'. The gossipy opening fits the confidence, but then
comes a moment of loss. He can go no further back than being
born, certainly not to the primal scene which would 'delve him
to the root', for the plot was lost some time before that, in his

father's death, memorialised in the gravestone, which functions in two ways.

First, however much 'compassion' DC says he felt, death permits an Oedipal structure, whereby, the father being buried, the bourgeois discards his past, and his history. The bourgeois hero, writing one year after the 1848 European revolutions, constructs his own modernity. 'Considered as a principle of life, modernity becomes a principle of origination,' Paul de Man writes, seeing modernity as what he calls 'radical renewal'.[2] The absence of the father, absence of origin, makes the child the originator of narrative. Hence the authority of the second chapter, 'I observe', which makes the boy's vision authorising, and which will be, by the end, a gaze from the centre of the Panopticon.[3] DC centres himself, and his memories – 'the memory of most of us can go further back into such times than many of us suppose . . . as a man I have a strong memory of my childhood' (2.21).

Yet – second – this narrative cannot be authoritative. The absence of an origin requires a supplementary origin and a supplementary narrative, for the episode is built around the discovery which the boy cannot register, since no-one lets him into the secret of the father, that his mother is being courted by Mr Murdstone, encountered in the illustration 'Our Pew At Church', before the moment of narrative diegesis. He observes the mother across the space of the picture, the width of the church. Murdstone suggests what price has to be paid for having buried the father. When the child hears, in the front parlour, where his father's body rested before being buried, about the resurrection of Lazarus, he has to be assured that the graves are 'at rest' (2.22). And when he hears that 'he has got a Pa', the prelude to being told that his mother has remarried, and married Mr Murdstone, the adult novelist says that 'something . . . connected with the grave in the churchyard, and the raising of the dead, seemed to strike me like an unwholesome wind' (3.48). As in *Hamlet*, the father's ghost walks momentarily, punishing the son's desires with Murdstone, the past coming back as another origin to finish posthumous existence. Merde: Murdstone: unwholesome wind. The excremental moment is repressed by the adult novelist (DC) in the recording of memory which leads up to the remarriage of Clara Copperfield, to evade questions of what David knew, and there is, rather, an imaginative writing leading up to the child's appalled excitement at finding himself dispossessed (the end of chapter 3). The claims for this as DC's 'written memory' (48.636) may be set aside as attempts to give authority to the text, so we return to other possibilities implied in the posthumous. The fascination of *David Copperfield* for reading the posthumous is how this undoes the text's confidence about its present: it gives the text allegorical status.

The father's return recalls Marx: 'men make their own history, but not of their own free will; not under circumstances they themselves have chosen but under the given and inherited circumstances with which they are directly confronted. The weight of the dead generations lies like a nightmare on the brains of the living.'[4] David Copperfield's narrative is called *The Personal History and Experience of David Copperfield the Younger*, so that David Copperfield the elder ghosts David Copperfield the younger, with his own lack of bourgeois success, his lack of survival and his naivety in relation to his marriage, which his aunt comments on, and which is repeated in the first marriage of David Copperfield the younger to Dora Spenlow. Repetition means that as with the double in Freud's essay 'The Uncanny', it is not just that the second must copy the first's identity, but that the first loses the distinctive quality of a separate identity. The posthumous must copy an original which he does not possess – but perhaps there was no original.

Murdstone is the usurper, whose imposition of identity threatens the child's own and makes his past recede further, and necessitates that it is denied. The crushing of the mother's recollections of her first husband, and her virtual disappearance, as though the past has been erased, belong here. The child must become his own father, and he constructs the father through literature: the father's 'small collection of books' which had been left upstairs in a small room adjoining his own. 'From that blessed little room, Roderick Random, Peregrine Pickle, Humphrey Clinker, Tom Jones, the Vicar of Wakefield, Don Quixote, Gil Blas and Robinson Crusoe came out, a glorious host, to keep me company' (3.59–60). The boy sits on the bed, 'reading as if for life'.

This legacy from the father gives DC no sense of historical alterity. Books, equated with characters, assume a posthumous status given by the child in the present, and all distance is cancelled out. The passage reads as an expropriation of the past-ness of the past through the confident present imagination; not surprisingly, Ruskin called Dickens a 'pure modernist', since for him, as for DC, the past exists only for use, and the choice of reading-matter is not accidental, for the prevalent theme of these texts is the male orphan growing up and searching for a father and an inheritance which are rightfully his, so that the past is reclaimed for the present, the boy in the present having demon-strated in his own terms his worthiness to receive his rightful legacy. This becomes a template for *David Copperfield*; the child is posthumous, but in another way not, because of the bourgeois confidence of a 'right' relation to the past.

That past is repressed, for DC identifies with 'a child's Tom Jones, a harmless creature', asserting that whatever 'harm' was in the books 'was not there for me: I knew nothing of it'. The passage intimates the knowledge of something other in the books than the child picked up, while denying either that the repres-sion involved in reading or that the knowledge that there was something to repress had any impact upon the child's or the narrator's subjectivity, formed on the basis of his reading.[5] The repression of the past texts, which is a repression of history, and which shows up in the child's ignorance of his mother's sexual appeal, leads to another, in the narrative: a repression of the text's present. DC as posthumous allows himself in on the father's secrets; the reading is his construction of the primal scene. There is no repression from the father, no father's no; while the adult novelist disavows the necessity for censorship, because the censor-ship that has already taken place is already more severe. It is the denial of anything in the past which the present might have diffi-culty in assimilating. Where the past has been so repressed, it becomes evident that the bourgeois can only speak of living on the basis of denial, which perhaps makes for an anxiety whether such living is possible. If reading negates the sexual so fully that 'I knew nothing of it', the experience of living has become cut off from experience.

2

The posthumous hero compelled to create his own origin speaks of two 'inheritances' due to him because of the time of his birth (midnight on Friday) – he will be unlucky, and he is destined to see ghosts and spirits (1.11). DC says that he has *not* seen ghosts and spirits, but this empiricist English consciousness while not acknowledging their existence, indeed repressing the meaning of ghosts into simply their most literal sense, nonetheless incorporates them into his prose, as in the words 'shadowy remembrance' (from the epigraph); he is ghosted by a past, implying a lack of control over the present.

DC has no time for ghosts, perhaps because of his modernity. He represses them out of an attitude towards the past, for 'I was a posthumous child' points to self-pity, permitting a certain 'narcissism of minor differences'[6] over others in this text whose fathers have died. (He also creates himself as posthumous in relation to the mother who dies with her new baby, DC's half-brother, remembering her as 'the young mother of my earliest impressions' and adding that 'the mother who lay in the grave, was the mother of my infancy, the little creature in her arms, was myself, as I had once been, hushed for ever on her bosom' (9.131). By identifying with the dead child, he makes his own living on posthumous.) At the heart of this, Dickens's first first-person narrative, is the question of how and how much to read the past. The subject tries to interpret those things which have made him what he is – but not sure what he is – and is anxious to control the self-presentation. Being the literal posthumous child allows for a dominant interpretation authorising a subjectivity whereby the past and the father the boy should have had reappears as Murdstone, who deprives the child of a past (this is doubled by the schoolmaster Creakle). When the boy is put to work in the factory in London through the stepfather's agency (chapters 11 and 12), the father reappears in parody form as Micawber, aspects of whose career – going to prison – follow Dickens's father, John Dickens. DC is looked after by the Micawber family, but, in a reversal of roles, he acts as a father to them and the 'Orfling' (orphan) working for them. When he walks to Dover to be cared for by Miss Trotwood, more fathers follow – Mr Dick, Dr Strong and Mr Wickfield – each chosen or choosing themselves for their lack of usurping/castrating power. Mr Spenlow, one of the last of the father-figures, is not an exception. These figures who will not threaten the present could each be taken as punishments of the father for having died, anger at the loss of the past.

The self-pity recalls a diagnosis Nietzsche makes in 'The Uses and Disadvantages of History for Life'. This essay begins reflecting on animals which live unhistorically, or ahistorically, contained wholly in the present. But the man, as opposed to the animal,

> says "I remember", and envies the animal, who all at once forgets and for whom every moment really dies. . . . [he learns to] . . . understand the phrase "it was": that password which gives conflict, suffering and satiety access to man so as to remind him what his existence fundamentally is – an imperfect tense that can never become a perfect one.[7]

In this, which identifies total forgetfulness with death, appears a phrase recurring in *Thus Spake Zarathustra*, to be discussed further in Part Three, implying that it is impossible to look at history without falling into *ressentiment*: the anguish that appears when it must be said '"It was"'. Paul de Man reads 'On the Uses and Disadvantages of History for Life' in terms of a tension between modernity and history:

> If history is not to become sheer regression or paralysis, it depends on modernity for its duration and renewal; but modernity cannot assert itself without being at once swallowed up and reintegrated into a regressive historical process . . . Modernity and history seem condemned to be linked together in a self-destroying union that threatens the survival of both. ('Literary History and Literary Modernity', 151)

History is the posthumous; as soon as modernity begins a relation to history, it too becomes posthumous. The posthumous child is free – and deprived; this appears first in the 'reflection' he has that his father never saw him. Taking the implications of this phrase, Lacan sees the ability to see an identity reflected in the mirror-state dependent upon having been already made the object of 'the gaze': i.e. by the look of the other, which frames subjectivity. DC has never been constructed by the father's gaze, and lacking this, other fathers (other forms of the past) have to come in; each of whom by attaining a quasi-patriarchal status are supplements to the father, filling his place in fantasy, as if each might be called David Copperfield the older. The structure of the text suggests that the subject's learning of himself as posthumous is not a single thing learned once for all; rather it creates a gap which has to be filled again and again, the filling of the gap being the text itself, a series of repeating fantasies, half plaint, and half self-construction. The lack of an origin provides the need to invent: DC attracts fathers and writes novels, another form of creating origins. The child tries to maintain an integrity with regard to having one origin, as when he is abandoned at the coach-station, with the guard asking if anyone will claim him, 'booked in the name of Murdstone . . . but owning to the name of Copperfield' (5.75), but even if he does that, the succession of father-figures only awakens the thought that all fatherhood, all the past is a form of usurpation intruding on the present.

3

David Copperfield the elder, the 'proper' father, withdraws as a 'natural' figure, as though the text also allows for another interpretation, where the father is no origin at all. Micawber becomes an alternative, a figure marked out by his living in language, as that which constructs his being. His literary language competes with the legacy of novels left to the son by the father; and they do not give that literature in a canonical, literary history form such as DC has been reading, but rather, as texts from the past only can be, co-existing in a vast, Borges-like anonymous text, a single library giving another, non-chronological history. He lives in and through letters, and contemplates dying into them, too, as when he finishes a letter reminding DC to come down to Canterbury, to assist at unmasking Uriah Heep:

> I trust I rendered tolerably intelligible my appointment for the morning of this day week at the house of public entertainment at Canterbury, where Mrs Micawber and myself had once the honour

of uniting our voices to yours, in the well-known strain of the immortal exciseman nurtured beyond the Tweed.

The duty done, and act of reparation performed, which can alone enable me to contemplate my fellow mortal, I shall be known no more. I shall simply require to be deposited in that place of universal resort where

> 'Each in his narrow cell for ever laid,
> The rude forefathers of the hamlet sleep,'

> – With the plain Inscription,
> WILKINS MICAWBER. (49.656)

Micawber's life here is made up of Burns's ('Auld Lang Syne') and Gray's 'Elegy Written in a Country Churchyard', and he contemplates his death along with all other fathers,[8] unadorned by any literature save the plain 'inscription', with which he signs the letter, and which he expects his grave to be signed. Writing the letter and the writing on the tomb – disseminatory ways in which the dead live on – are the same; anticipating an inscription written posthumously he looks beyond death, and, since this is not his last letter, he also – naturally – looks forward to another life after trying out being dead.[9]

Micawber, figure of non-origins, goes into prison, in a 'narrow cell' before the final one that he anticipates, while DC works at Murdstone and Grinby's factory in London. Micawber petitions Parliament, praying for an alteration in the law of imprisonment for debt, and DC says something of his memory of the prisoners coming to sign this petition – relevant for consideration of the non-Micawber-like way in which he interprets:

> I set down the remembrance here, because it is an instance to myself of the manner in which I fitted my old books to my altered life, and made stories for myself, out of the streets, and out of men and women; and how some main points in the character I shall unconsciously develop, I suppose, in writing my life, were gradually forming all this while.

> As I walked to and fro daily between Southwark and Blackfriars, and lounged about at meal-times in obscure streets, the stones of which may, for anything I know, be worn at this moment by my childish feet, I wonder how many of these people were wanting in the crowd that used to come filing before me in review again [prisoners in the

66

King's Bench prison], to the echo of Captain Hopkins's voice [a
particular prisoner]. When my thoughts go back, now, to that slow
agony of my youth, I wonder how much of the histories I invented
for such people hangs like a mist of fancy over well-remembered
facts! When I tread the old ground, I do not wonder that I seem to
see and pity, going on before me, an innocent romantic boy, making
his imaginative world out of such strange experiences and sordid
things. (11.164, 165)[10]

In the first extract, the books read beforehand, reminders of the
father, live on in their application to people met with in the
London streets and the prison (these things are the same), while
the future tense 'the character I shall unconsciously develop, I
suppose, in writing my life' opens up the topic of what life it is
that DC as the author of this personal history is developing. When
he admits to feeling unhappy with his marriage to Dora Spenlow
(though this may be too strong a way of putting it), he adds that
'what I am describing, slumbered, and half awoke, and slept
again, in the innermost recesses of my mind. There was no
evidence of it in me; I know of no influence it had in anything
I said or did' (48.643). The disavowal that he made Dora unhappy
– three paragraphs before Dora's imminent death becomes
apparent – points to the text's uncertainty about what a text, like
a person's conscious and unconscious actions, says when it does
not say something. DC, in chapter 11, means by his 'character'
the one he 'develops' within the text – knowing that the textual
life survives the death of the author and becomes other, but not
aware of what textual unconscious will appear. He also knows
that the writing of the text will change him in the future. The
text will gain a posthumous existence; the text will also become
his father. Interpretation of the past is not settled; he does not
know what connects with what; the past cannot be left because
he is not certain what he is in the present – what the uncertain
past has made him.

He thinks also of a doubled existence: the stones of the streets
are worn by his feet as though he as a ghost were walking them 'at
this moment', while he as a man is writing. As he walked as a child,
so all the figures of the prison came before him in review again,
in another doubled existence. Writing 'now', he wonders what was
true in his memory of those figures and what he supplemented

through the figures of eighteenth-century literature: creating another form of posthumous existence, whereby people are seen not as what they are, but as representations of the past. 'Treading the old ground' is the activity of an adult writer walking in London, or of a ghost/writer, and in whatever form he does it, he sees 'an innocent romantic boy, making his imaginative world out of . . . strange experiences and sordid things'. The boy goes on before, the Ghost leading Hamlet, father to the man the novelist, but a figure summoned up in an act of prosopopoeia as innocent, and to be pitied.

The character unconsciously developed is filled with *ressentiment*, just as the imagination of the child – with which the adult DC sympathises – inscribes the figures of the prison with the features of the past out of a form of *ressentiment*, as though the past were needed as a supplement to the present. Micawber lives in the present, with virtually no recall of the past, at one instant 'making motions at himself with a razor; but within half an hour afterwards, he would polish up his shoes with extraordinary pains, and go out, humming a tune with a greater air of gentility than before' (11.155). His risk is total disconnection: his career would have to be read through Deleuze and Guattari's 'schizoanalysis', having no sense of a single subject entity. Another letter makes the point; its literariness scattering identity, while its topic is that he is being legally challenged (the law assumes a fixed identity) and he expects to lose out to Heep and the law:

> Consigned to which, and to a speedy end (for mental torture is not supportable beyond a certain point, and that point I feel I have attained), my course is run. Bless you, bless you! Some future traveller, visiting, from motives of curiosity, not unmingled, let us hope, with sympathy, the place of confinement allotted to debtors in this city, may, and I trust will, Ponder, as he traces on its wall, inscribed with a rusty nail,
>
> The obscure initials
> W.M.
>
> P.S. I reopen this to say that our common friend, Mr Thomas Traddles (who has not yet left us and is looking extremely well) has paid the debt and costs, in the noble name of Miss Trotwood; and that myself and family are at the height of earthly bliss. (54.720–1)

Child and father together, he anticipates two deaths – suicide and death in prison, and so a double marginalisation putting him outside history; he anticipates a future beyond the grave where his initials will be a question for interpretation; he writes a subscript which makes the main script superfluous, only he has forgotten that, and the postscript anticipates a future where he is posthumous, where the 'traveller' engaged in the act of prosopopoeia is likely to find that resurrection has already taken place.

In contrast to this interpretive freedom, DC needs a particular version of the past to live in the present. Though a modern, he feels the poverty of the present, so that as an adult novelist, he also lives not by his now present, but by the past of the boy, so that he pities himself as he was.

4

'I was a posthumous child' is at the heart of Dickens. Oliver Twist was posthumous, but in *Oliver Twist*, chapter 51, he discovers what his father thought, did and said in his last illness; so that the past is given back to him. Accordingly, he is not said to be posthumous; he is not, at the end, marooned in relation to the past. Because it deprives the subject of an origin, so that it is not the origin of anything in itself, but rather points to the posthumous nature of being throughout, the character of the posthumous is to open up a gap, a melancholia like an 'open wound', as Freud says.[11] The rest of the text rushes in and fails to close this wound. Other forms of anguish follow, as for example:

> I now approach a period of my life, which I can never lose the remembrance of, while I remember anything; and the recollection of which has often, without my invocation, come before me like a ghost, and haunted happier times. (10.147)

This from the writer who says he has never seen ghosts! – in a denial of his own melancholia and *ressentiment*. Now, however, as a contented bourgeois writer, he looks back on his past 'happier times' and he denies their fulness insofar as the 'recollection' of the days working in the factory come up at those times. The locution 'I can never lose . . . while I remember anything' is a performative; it is a willing not to forget, a melancholic return to time's 'it was'.

DC reminds us of another writer describing working in the blacking-factory, whom I now quote:

> My whole nature was so penetrated with the grief and humiliation . . . that even now, famous, caressed and happy, I often forget in my dreams that I have a dear wife and children; even that I am a man; and wander desolately back to that time of my life.[12]

This is Dickens, describing in an autobiographical fragment his hard labour at the age of twelve in London, while his father was in prison. He did not publish the fragment but passed it to his biographer, John Forster, for posthumous publication, by making sure it would be included in Forster's *Life of Charles Dickens*, two years after his own death. Dickens seems to have thought of the posthumous from at least the time of *The Posthumous Papers of the Pickwick Club*. In a *mise en abîme*, one of the planned Copperfield titles runs *The Last Living Speech and Confessions of David Copperfield, Junior, of Blunderstone Lodge, Who Was Never Executed at the Old Bailey. Being his Personal History Found Among His Papers*. Since DC says that 'this manuscript is intended for no eyes but mine' (47.559) – the split subject talking – it is to be assumed that publication, if any, is to be posthumous. The title inscribes the posthumous in two different forms, making posthumous publication the norm.

5

Dickens possessed in his library a copy of the posthumously published works of Thomas Chatterton, Wordsworth's 'lovely boy, the sleepless soul that perished in his pride' ('Resolution and Independence'), and possible model if only in that detail for Steerforth, even though the class-relationships are different. Meredith modelled a feminine-looking Chatterton for Henry

Wallis's *The Death of Chatterton* in 1856, so constructing for the Victorians a softened romantic poet. But Chatterton, who was born 20 November 1752, and killed himself in London on 24 August 1770, could have been a model for DC, being also posthumous. The elder Thomas Chatterton, born in 1713, died on 7 August 1752. A first son had already died. Chatterton senior had been a schoolmaster and musician at Bristol's St Mary Redcliff; it also seems that he brought home old papers from the church, just as his son forged, from his twelfth year onwards, old documents which he claimed to have found there, and said had been written by the fictitious fifteenth-century poet and priest Sir Thomas Rowley.

Are there connections between being posthumous – which gives a form of freedom from history – and inventing history, as Chatterton invented that of medieval Bristol? Or being posthumous and in rooting among the father's papers – as if hoping to establish a past through them, and creating that past by creating new papers? Was it a hope to do something with the fragmentary, with the detritus of history? Was the young Chatterton trying to be his father? It was not enough that Chatterton wrote poetry which Coleridge, Wordsworth, Blake, Southey, Keats and Byron all admired; it had to be given a fictitious ancestry; the Rowley poems would not appear under Chatterton's own name. What connections may be made between being posthumous, writing, and forging? Pip's occupation in *Great Expectations* seems to glance at the connection, if Pip is to be taken as posthumous;[13] while Stephen Dedalus plays on the connection between a fictitious father whose identity is established through a patronymic and writing:

> Welcome O life! I go . . . to forge in the smithy of my soul the uncreated conscience of my race . . . Old father, old artificer, stand me now and ever in good stead.[14]

Is it enough to say that writing, as an unfathered activity, destroys the authenticity that a concept such as forgery tries to create? If writing was a libidinal action for Chatterton, how does this compare with DC, and what is to be said of the failure of the free spirit in his suicide? Is it the father's punishment? What connection is there between Chatterton's suicide and his response to his father? One short piece published by Chatterton in January 1770, 'The Unfortunate Fathers', shows the son, crossed in love by his father (mercenary, parochial and middle class), and shooting himself, leaving this note behind:

> I shall not accuse your conduct, for you are my father; I shall only endeavour to vindicate the action I am about to perpetrate. This will easily be done. There is a principle in man . . . which constitutes him the image of God . . . if a man acts according to this regulator, he is right, if contrary to it, he is wrong. It is an approved truth, that this principle varies in every rational being. As I can reconcile suicide to this principle, with me it is consequently no crime. Suicide is sometimes a noble insanity of the soul: and often the result of a mature and deliberate approbation of the soul. If ever a crime, it is only so to society: there indeed it always appears an irrational emotion: but when our being becomes dissocial, when we neither assist nor are assisted by society, we do not injure it by laying down our load of life.[15]

The fictitious father's death follows before three months are out; suicide seems to act retrospectively on the father, cancelling out his paternity, destroying him.

It seems that Chatterton is an alternative to David Copperfield, who rises to bourgeois success, starting at a good school in *his* twelfth year, and sorting out the Dictionary papers of his schoolmaster surrogate father, Dr Strong, before he becomes a successful novelist himself. The novel's playful tone for its draft titles, implying fictionality and criminality – others include *The Copperfield Disclosures* (secrets to be revealed), and *The Last Will and Testament of Mr David Copperfield. Being his Personal History left as a Record* (legal, and assuring his own paternity will be remembered), shows the text's awareness that the Chatterton experience could have been more likely, and that the reading of the father's books, like Chatterton with his father's papers, shows what the fate of the posthumous is also likely to be. Chatterton's posthumous existence was to become the romantic hero. What guilt and repression were entailed in throwing this destiny off from David Copperfield on to Steerforth? The posthumous state is the *pharmakon* – a gift, liberation from patriarchy, but also poison, imaged in the arsenic Chatterton took.[16]

6

The novel appears after the death of its author, David Copperfield. *David Copperfield* seems posthumous itself, as though it embodied the reality of the novelist's being. As Dickens finished, so he wrote to Forster, 'I am within three pages of the shore, and am strangely divided, as usual in such cases, between sorrow and joy. Oh, my dear Forster, if I were to say half of what Copperfield makes me feel tonight, how strangely, even to you, I should be turned inside-out! I seem to be sending some part of myself into the Shadowy World.'[17]

The 'Shadowy World' is the future, but the letter implies that finishing the novel is part of becoming posthumous. It is not the novel which turns him inside-out by revealing his secret existence; the relationship between him and the text which probes him, searches him; either creating him a new figure by the writing of the text, or destroying him. In his notes for the novel (the number-plans) he wrote of the episode in the factory, 'What I know so well' – meaning that it was memory that had never been discarded, but gone over repeatedly. The glimpses of Dickens imply a deep and 'secret melancholy' openly confessed to as an abiding source of unhappiness in the lead-character. The bourgeois cannot believe his own success story, though he can write it. It makes the bourgeois *Bildungsroman* secretly a text of violence. Dickens can say that he forgets he has a wife, under the impact of memory of the past trauma, but DC goes one better; since when it becomes evident that the marriage to Dora Spenlow will not work, the logic of the text (which has already permitted the thought that the child has killed the father) allows the wife to die, so freeing DC both for a mourning in which melancholia is not present and for remarriage.

But there is a gap between Dickens and DC. In Dickens, it is sufficient justification of the bitterness and anger (even though he says 'I do not write resentfully or angrily' – Forster, 35) that he had been deserted to the blacking-factory. With DC, that is only supplementary to another desertion, or rather, it seems that desertion is endless, for to delve DC to the root would be to go back to the primary loss, or loss as primary. The implicit confession of *ressentiment* does not have an origin; it lies in a past that cannot be accessed. Each act of DC, starting away from his discovery of being posthumous, while appearing to give him a future, also deepens his perception of that prime act of being posthumous, so that he is always writing about his past, going further back, even as the narrative of the novel moves forward.

7

In 'The Uses and Disadvantages of History for Life', Nietzsche, noting how certain things in the past are unchallengeable, tries to look at the past without *ressentiment*:

> The best we can do is to confront our inherited and hereditary nature with our knowledge of it, and through a new, stern discipline combat our inborn heritage and implant in ourselves a new habit, a new instinct, a second nature so that our first nature withers away. It is an attempt to give oneself, a posteriori, a past in which one would like to originate in opposition to that in which one did originate: – always a dangerous attempt because it is so hard to know the limit to denial of the past . . . here and there a victory is nonetheless achieved, and for the combatants, for those who employ critical history for the sake of life, there is even a noteworthy consolation: that of knowing that this first nature was once a second nature and that every victorious second nature will become a first. (76–7)[18]

The 'noteworthy consolation' is a startling form of changing the past, where the primary and original turns out to be not so but a palimpsest overlaying something else; there is no fixed nature and no fixed past, and the powerful hegemonic reading of reality, under which the subject feels cowed or threatened, is only a reading superimposed on another.

In this, Nietzsche anticipates Freud, in the analysis of the Wolf-man (Sergei Pankeev, 1879–1979), whom he treated for four years, till 1914, and wrote about in *From the History of an Infantile Neurosis*. Can we connect David Copperfield with the Wolf-man? For Freud liked *David Copperfield*, giving it to Martha Bernays before their marriage, and telling her in a letter (5 October 1883) that it was the most free of mannerisms of those of Dickens

74

he had read: 'the characters are individualized; they are sinful without being abominable'.[19] One slight point to link *David Copperfield* and this analysis: both DC and the Wolf-man were born with a caul (an inheritance from the mother, a trace of the posthumous related to the mother). The Wolf-man, Freud says, 'had for that reason always looked upon himself as a special child of fortune whom no ill could befall . . . the caul was the veil which hid him from the world and hid the world from him'.[20] The 'caul' is the sign of luck: *Glückshaube*, 'lucky hood'. In DC's case, the bad luck he was threatened with and the good luck from the caul (but the caul can only be good luck when it is removed) cancel each other out.

One strategy in Freud's analysis compares with Nietzsche. Freud considered that the dream the Wolf-man described having when he was four – of the white wolves sitting on the branches of the walnut tree in front of the window – was an 'activation (I purposely avoid the word "recollection")' of a 'primal scene' witnessed when he was one and a half, even though 'the effects of the scene were deferred' (276–7). As a delayed reaction, the dream worked over the material of the primal scene. It seemed to point to an earlier reality – which Freud also conceded might be a fantasy. While the Wolf-man had no remembrance of such a primal scene, Freud thought its impact was felt as a deferred action (*Nachträglichkeit*), a deferred understanding (278, 293). He did not think it likely that such a remembrance could appear other than as a 'construction' (284, 285), a present invention, making the past appear in a certain way. To offer such a remembrance to a patient as a construction makes the past different, something that the person may now feel he or she can live with. The interpretation, according to Nietzsche, has changed, for what is there but interpretation?

> The actual causes of a thing's origin and its eventual uses, the manner of its incorporation into a system of purposes, are worlds apart . . . everything that exists, no matter what its origin, is periodically reinterpreted by those in power in terms of fresh intentions . . . all processes in the organic world are processes of outstripping and overcoming, and . . . in turn, all outstripping and overcoming means reinterpretation, rearrangement, in the course of which the earlier meaning and purpose are necessarily either lost or obscured . . .

> Thus the whole history of a thing, an organ, a custom, becomes a
> constant chain or reinterpretations and rearrangements which need
> not be causally connected among themselves, which may simply
> follow one another.[21]

Events in the past exist as interpretations that have been successful;
indeed, it is hardly possible to sort out which is the event and
which the interpretation, and the hope in making an interpretation is in its becoming 'victorious'.

The image of the tree in the Wolf-man's dream itself pulls
back thought to the notion of origins and of the family tree, as
in *Cymbeline*. It has been argued that working with current pictures
of the family tree and the Darwinian tree of mankind, Freud
read the Wolf-man's drawing of his dream as 'the psychic history
of mankind – child, infant, family and species'.[22] This would
imply the danger of pulling thought back to a singular origin
and would echo Deleuze and Guattari, that 'the tree has domi-
nated Western reality, and all of Western thought', when
discussing the dangers of arborescent thought – which attempts
to unify origins and divisions, working on the basis of 'a centred
or segmented higher unity'.

> Arborescent systems are hierarchical systems with centres of signifiance
> and subjectification, central automata like organised memories.

In contrast, Deleuze and Guattari propose rhizomic thought,
which is an 'antigenealogy' (with no family trees) and 'always
detachable, connectable, reversible, modifiable, and [which] has
multiple entryways and exits and its own lines of flight'.[23] David
Copperfield and Freud think back, interpretively, towards a
history with a single origin: the father, the primal scene.

8

Derrida writes, in 'Freud and the Scene of Writing', on those
moments in Freud which counter the logocentric. Concepts of
Nachträglichkeit and *Verspätung* (delay) do much more than just
promoting such single and linear interpretations. According to
Derrida, they 'govern the whole of Freud's thought and determine

all his other concepts . . . the irreducibility of the "effect of deferral" – such, no doubt, is Freud's discovery'.[24] Delay, deferred reaction, repetition imply Derrida's 'reserve':

> Is it not already death at the origin of a life which can defend itself against death only through an economy of death, through deferrment, repetition, reserve? (202)

The passage, a reminder of Derrida's Hegelianism, in its stress on death, might be a commentary on *David Copperfield* and on the necessity of the posthumous, as it picks its way through Freud, refusing to put life and death into a binary opposition, rather indicating that death works through a system, necessary to it, in order to (p)reserve the organism's life. Life shields itself from the impact of a threatening presence, and posthumous effects work throughout life. A primary inscription on the psyche already meets the resistance of memory, so that memory is part of the reserve. Memory relates to the 'trace', the writing already within the subject, whose existence means that:

> [T]here is no life present at first which would then come to protect, postpone, or reserve itself in *différance*. The latter constitutes the essence of life. Or rather, as *différance* is not an essence, as it is not anything, it is not life, if Being is determined as *ousia* [Being], presence, essence, existence, substance or subject. Life must be thought of as trace before Being may be determined as presence. (203)

Derrida draws support from the deconstructive moment in Freud's *Interpretation of Dreams* where primariness is called a 'theoretical fiction'.[25] The delay is in the beginning, or we may think of beginnings as posthumous, any beginning lacking entitlement to become an origin, the origin of narrative. Derrida continues:

> To defer (*différer*) thus cannot mean to retard a present possibility, to postpone an act, to put off a perception already now possible. That possibility is possible only through a *différance* which must be conceived of in other terms than those of a calculus or mechanics of decision. To say that *différance* is originary is simultaneously to erase the myth of a present origin. Which is why 'originary' must be understood as having been crossed out, without which *différance*

would be derived from an original plenitude. It is a non-origin which is originary. (203)

Something within the present belongs to an undecidable, unascertainable past; a 'present' memory – but for Derrida there cannot be a memory which is present, which belongs punctually to a given moment – memories cannot be located as relating to a past moment, with simply the force of a decision on the part of the critic, deciding on what is past and what is present. Memories are posthumous, in the sense that they cannot be linked to a father; they are rootless. If the novel claims to be 'written memory', we may say that memory is already written as a form of resistance to such writing, as the pre-existent trace in the subject, its existence as such guessed at when the child reads the archive of English literature, and can make such an easy identification with it.

Freud's procedure with the 'Rat Man', in 'Notes upon a Case of Obsessional Neurosis' (1909), is similar to that with the Wolf-man, and equally exploits the non-relationship between memories. He deduced that the patient had been soundly punished by his father for auto-erotic behaviour when he was six; the patient then returned to Freud at a subsequent session with the detail his mother had told him that he had been beaten by his father when he was younger. He had no recollection of this.

> The patient subsequently questioned his mother again. She confirmed the story, adding that at the time he had been between three and four years old and that he had been given the punishment because he had bitten some one. She could remember no further details . . . in her account there was no suggestion of his misdeed having been of a sexual nature.[26]

The Rat Man refused to believe that he had ever broken out in fury against his father (as Freud had previously deduced) even in the teeth of this new evidence.

> And so it was only along the painful road of transference that he was able to reach a conclusion that his relation to his father really necessitated the postulation of this unconscious complement. (89)

The memory must be supplemented; the patient's past becomes

a choice of interpretations – Freud's and his own, but there is no 'right' choice.

Did Freud in his work on the Rat Man recollect David Copperfield biting Mr Murdstone (4.62)? In biting, DC proves what Mr Murdstone has already said of him, 'somebody's sharp' (2.31) – though as both memories exist in DC's mind as he writes, it must remain a question to what extent these two things can be aligned in a linear order – and the whole episode in Dickens, if remembered by Freud would then beg the question what things in DC have not been said, what 'reserve' of memories remains undisclosed. In the context of the Rat Man biting someone, Freud writes about the 'consolidation' of childhood memories which 'involves a complicated process of remodelling, analogous in every way to the process by which a nation constructs legends about its early history' (86–7, n. 2). This recalls *Cymbeline*; the nation and the young adult construct similar narratives to give themselves a firm and single identity (and the adult male's construction of identity is also the attempt at construction of a national identity). Freud adds that in constructing memories, these become sexualised and involve seductions and assaults from others, effacing their auto-erotic character: the construction of fantasies means that 'he brings commonplace experiences into relation with his sexual activity, and extends his sexual interest to them – though in doing this he is probably following upon the traces [*Spuren*] of a really existing connection'. He leaves it an open question whether the punishment for biting someone had anything to do with sexual misdeeds. The fictional DC, born somewhere in the early nineteenth century, compares with the Rat Man, born in 1878, Freud's creation, and inserted into an attempted *Bildungsroman* as Freud writes about him that having been cured, 'like so many other young men of value and promise, he perished in the Great War' (128: footnote added in 1923).

Freud's statement draws on the 'trace', and for Derrida, in his essay '*Différance*', that has to do with a past that has never been present; for 'one cannot think the trace . . . on the basis of the present, or the presence of the present'. By 'the trace', Derrida means another text: and, as in the essay '*Ousia* and *Gramme*':

in order to exceed metaphysics, it is necessary that a trace be inscribed within the text of metaphysics, a trace that continues to signal . . . in the direction of an entirely other text.[27]

The trace not only does away with self-apparent origins, but thinking in relation to it opens up how a textual system is contaminated by other texts. DC becomes aware of unattributable feelings. Shocked by Uriah Heep's declaration to him of love towards Agnes, appalled by the thought of her contamination by 'this red-headed animal', he writes:

> He seemed to swell and grow before my eyes; the room seemed full of the echoes of his voice, and the strange feeling (to which, perhaps, no one is quite a stranger) that all this had happened before, at some indefinite time, and that I knew what he was going to say next, took possession of me. (25. 355–6)

Delayed reaction – but to what? It signals, possibly, to some part of the text; but does not suggest that this will lead to a single right reading. The memories running through it cannot be confined to DC; or even, given the name-changes, to a single boy. To read a text of the past is to realise that several are being read, several possibilities ghosting each text, none of them necessarily embodying experiences which were ever fully present.

9

I now approach an event in my life, so indelible, so awful, so bound by an infinite variety of ties to all that has preceded it, in these pages, that, from the beginning of my narrative, I have seen it growing larger and larger as I advanced, like a great tower in a plain, and throwing its forecast shadow even on the incidents of my childish days.

For years after it occurred, I dreamed of it often. I have started up so vividly impressed by it, that its fury has yet seemed raging in my quiet room, in the still night. I dream of it, sometimes, though at lengthened and uncertain intervals, to this hour. I have an association between it and a stormy wind, or the lightest mention of a sea-shore, as strong as any of which my mind is conscious. As plainly as I beheld what happened, I will try to write it down. I do not recall it, but see it done, for it happens again before me. (55.721)

Who could have guessed that *this* writing, living on posthumously in the hero long after the event, would appear in *David Copperfield* after its first fifty-four chapters? The novelist (DC) who has invoked first the trauma of being posthumous and then of the factory and escape from it to Dover, now turns in a way which seems incompatible with those experiences, and in an anamorphotic passage which does not seem to relate to these others, or with much else of the bourgeois experience of the novel, locates trauma elsewhere. The text becomes like a detective novel where the centre of attention turns out to be other from the way it had been narrated. It asks for nearly the whole novel, with only nine chapters left, to be re-read for the signs of what is to happen in this chapter – such as 'the sea roars as if it were hungry for us' – (Steerforth, 21.291). It reinvests with significance the caul of the novel's beginning, which had implied freedom from drowning, where that meant freedom from engulfment, from loss of identity, from dissolution, from being eaten. It recalls the old empty rooks' nests, which 'swung like wrecks upon a stormy sea' (1.15). Chapter 55, 'Tempest', gives the drowning of Steerforth, the seducer of Emily, another man without a father, washed up, posthumously, lying on the shore in a foetal position (but with no caul), so completing the sense of the chapter-title, 'I am born', where being born is being dead (while 'borne' on the waves is also a pun at work in this chapter). Suddenly, the name 'Steerforth' no longer possesses an obviously questionable dark sense, in referring to the man who steers forth, as if with the death-drive, his sexuality cutting its way through all waters (just as he threw the hammer to cut Rosa Dartle, in contrast to the way that 'Brooks of Sheffield' who is sharp, does not cut, even if he bites). The name is no longer a charmed thing. The passage in recalling Steerforth's centrality also enables a realisation that DC ghosts him – as he hints when David comes upon him 'like a reproachful ghost' (22.301).

The opening of the chapter articulates the narrative differently from the way it had gone before, changing its nodal points of trauma, with the suggestion that earlier traumas find their fulfilment here. Does this, which has opened up a new trauma which survives into the present and has made the writing of the past difficult in the knowledge that it must lead to it, activate analeptically the writing of the earlier experiences, informing their desolation with the trace of something else? If, as an episode, it has not finished: 'it happens again before me', so it haunts what has been written earlier. As such, it requires a re-reading of the first line, 'whether I shall turn out to be the hero of my own life, or whether that station will be held by anybody else, these pages must show'. The implicit open question is answered as the posthumous child has identified with another whom he has installed as the hero of his life, as though Steerforth were a fulfilment of the Tom Jones he found among his father's books and whom he attempted to embody. Drowning this hero sets up a figure in the text in whom an enormous emotional investment can be made (DC 'warming his shivering hands with a death'). But then it is like a castration, a disenchantment of the world, making all existence posthumous. The person whom we took to be the hero becomes the substitute, and the narrative of his confident progress which we had taken as an allegory of the novelist, points towards another narrative which it cannot quite know, which has been consistently moved beyond reach, but which now intersects with the experience of DC. Perhaps part of the horror felt in the opening of this chapter comes from guilt at feeling that he has given to another the free-thinking, libidinal Chatterton-like qualities he himself disavows, and that the price of that is the death of the other; another death, to add to Dora's. The caul which saved him is the *pharmakon*, but it is also his death, making the bourgeois inert while successful, as though transferring the revolutionary qualities which the working class posthumous hero (Chatterton) possessed (posthumous since the working class are excluded from history) on to the aristocrat, who also can only have a posthumous existence within the pages of *David Copperfield*.[28]

Although the narrative is, as always, of desire, here it includes the frustration that it is not wholly one of bourgeois success, and although the tower-image's phallicism leads towards the emotional contest between DC and Steerforth for Emily, where the phallic mastery – but not bourgeois success – has been conceded to Steerforth. The passage indicates, as if against Lacan, that the semiotic functions of language do not necessarily relate back to the father. The event has ties with other events, but which ones? *Nachträglichkeit* does not support one narrative, but multiple ones: the text of David Copperfield indicates desire which is powerful in linking with other objects, being rhizomic, not only arborescent. We may see *David Copperfield* as investigating how many ways a psyche can know the past and the present, when both are knowable only as textual. Mr Micawber's language is *mise en abîme* within this larger scene of writing; it includes it, and everything else. David Copperfield asks how aspects of textuality may be linked when memories are not reconcilable with each other, and even the narrator's sense of what traumatises him cannot quite be allowed to stand.

The hero's undecidable status in relation to Dickens mirrors the text's creator's relation to his own past – how much has this, and how much has the text created him? – and it is repeated by the hero's puzzlement about his relation to his past, and in relation to Steerforth as something other within and ghosting his narrative. When Dickens felt that in completing the novel he was sending out part of himself into the shadowy world, that has to do with the perception of having produced a text, whose character means that it is neither present nor past, which he himself could hardly know his way about, and link point to point. The structures of the Victorian novel, stopping and starting over twenty months, in a structure of repetition whose gaps act as the reserve, making a single narrative of the life impossible, have led to the end of a narrative where there is so much that the plot or the visible ligaments of the novel cannot explain. Being posthumous means coming too late for comprehension, and is a trope for feeling a lack of comprehensibility.

Notes

1. Dickens, *David Copperfield,* ed. Jeremy Tambling (Harmondsworth: Penguin, 1996), p. 12.
2. Paul de Man, 'Literary History and Literary Modernity', in *Blindness and Insight: Essays on the Rhetoric of Contemporary Criticism* (Minneapolis: University of Minnesota Press, 1983), p. 150.
3. On this, see my 'Carlyle in Prison: Reading Latter-Day Pamphlets', *Dickens Studies Annual* 26 (1997), 311–33. David Copperfield, in chapter 61, visits the Model Prison (probably Pentonville) which was laid out on Panoptical lines (cf. the work of Foucault on the Panopticon, in *Discipline and Punish*). See my *Dickens, Violence and the Modern State* (London: Macmillan, 1995) for discussions of the relevance of Foucault to study of Dickens.
4. Marx, *The Eighteenth Brumaire of Louis Bonaparte,* in *Surveys from Exile,* ed. David Fernbach (Harmondsworth: Penguin, 1973), p. 146.
5. On the importance of childhood perception here, see Franco Moretti, *The Way of the World: The Bildungsroman in European Culture* (London: Verso, 1987), pp. 181–214.
6. Freud, 'Civilisation and its Discontents', *The Penguin Freud, 12: Civilisation, Society and Religion* (Harmondsworth: Penguin, 1985), p. 305.
7. Nietzsche, 'The Uses and Disadvantages of History for Life', in *Untimely Observations,* trans. R. J. Hollingdale, introduction by Daniel Breazeale (Cambridge: Cambridge University Press, 1997), p. 61.
8. The 'rude forefathers' contrast with Gray's 'youth to fortune and to fame unknown'. His epitaph – that of the poet's, whom the poem addresses as 'thee', as though imagining his death, and making itself posthumous in relation to its father, since the poem cannot be completed before the father's death – appears at the end of Gray's 'Elegy Written in a Country Churchyard'. The poem posits poetic existence – its own and Gray's – as posthumous: the dead youth is unnamed by any father. The death of the youth compares with Collins's 'Dirge in "Cymbeline"' (1744), a rewriting of Shakespeare's

dirge for the unfathered youth – Fidele – whose death becomes a new point of origin for country life; see the edition of Collins, ed. Richard Wendorf and Charles Ryskamp (Oxford: Clarendon Press, 1979), pp. 21–2. Graveyard poetry seems dedicated to the posthumous and the without-posterity.

9. This could be compared with Melquíades in Gabriel García Marquez' *One Hundred Years of Solitude,* who after dying 'had returned because he could not bear the solitude', trans. Gregory Rabassa (Harmondsworth: Penguin, 1972), p. 50.

10. On this passage, see Ned Lukacher, *Primal Scenes: Literature, Philosophy, Psychoanalysis* (Ithaca: Cornell University Press, 1986), pp. 317–21 specifically.

11. Freud, 'Mourning and Melancholia', *The Penguin Freud,* 11 (Harmondsworth: Penguin, 1977), p. 262.

12. John Forster, *Life of Charles Dickens,* ed. J. W. T. Ley (London: Cecil Palmer, 1928), p. 26.

13. Pip has had five brothers all dead, none of whom he remembers, so presumably he was the youngest. That he is posthumous is not stated, but in contrast to his brothers, he is named for his father; he is Philip Pirrip the younger, emphasising the father-relation. See my 'Writing Epitaphs: Narrative in *Great Expectations*', in *Great Expectations: Charles Dickens,* ed. Jean-Pierre Naugrette (Paris: Ellipses, 1999), pp. 141–52.

14. James Joyce, *A Portrait of the Artist as a Young Man* (1916; London: Jonathan Cape, 1987), p. 228.

15. Thomas Chatterton, *Complete Works,* ed. Donald S. Taylor and Benjamin B. Hoover, 2 vols (Oxford: Clarendon Press, 1971), vol. 1, pp. 445–6. On Chatterton, see Louise J. Kaplan, *The Family Romance of the Impostor-Poet, Thomas Chatterton* (New York: Athenenaum, 1988): while informative I find its psychoanalysis overly predictable. Kaplan concludes that Chatterton died of melancholia (pp. 213–35). See also Susan Stewart, *Crimes of Writing: Problems in the Containment of Representation* (North Carolina: Duke University Press, 1994), chapter 5.

16. For the *pharmakon* (poison and medicine), see Derrida,

'Plato's Pharmacy', in *Dissemination,* trans. Barbara Johnson (Chicago: University of Chicago Press, 1981).

17. Letter, 21 October 1850, *The Pilgrim Edition* (Oxford: Clarendon Press, 1988), p. 195.

18. On this passage, see the essay by Alexander Nehemas, 'The Genealogy of Genealogy: Interpretation in Nietzsche's Second *Untimely Meditation* and in *The Genealogy of Morals*', in Richard Schacht (ed.), *Nietzsche, Genealogy, Morality: Essays on Nietzsche's Genealogy of Morals* (Berkeley: University of California Press, 1994), pp. 269–83. I discuss this text further in Part Three.

19. Quoted, Ernest Jones, *The Life and Work of Sigmund Freud* (New York: Basic Books, 1967), vol. 1, p. 174; see also p. 104.

20. 'From the History of an Infantile Neurosis', *Case Histories, 2; The Penguin Freud Library,* vol. 9 (Harmondsworth: Penguin, 1979), p. 340.

21. Nietzsche, *The Genealogy of Morals,* II.xii, trans. Francis Golffing (New York: Doubleday Anchor, 1956), pp. 209–10. Douglas Smith in his translation (Oxford: World's Classics, 1996) speaks of a 'chain of signs, of ever new interpretations and manipulations' (p. 58). The German is 'Zeichen-Kette'. See below, p. 166.

22. Whitney Davis, *Drawing the Dream of the Wolves: Homosexuality, Interpretation and Freud's 'Wolf Man'* (Bloomington: University of Indiana Press, 1995), p. 182.

23. Gilles Deleuze and Félix Guattari, *A Thousand Plateaus: Capitalism and Schizophrenia,* trans. Brian Massumi (London: Athlone Press, 1988), pp. 18, 16, 21.

24. Derrida, 'Freud and the Scene of Writing', *Writing and Difference,* trans. Alan Bass (London: Routledge, 1978), p. 203.

25. The passage in Freud is *The Interpretation of Dreams,* in *The Penguin Freud,* vol. 4 (Harmondsworth: Penguin, 1976), p. 763.

26. *The Penguin Freud,* vol. 9, pp. 85–6.

27. Derrida, *Margins of Philosophy,* trans. Alan Bass (London: Harvester Press, 1982), pp. 21, 65. For these thoughts on the trace, see Robert Bernasconi, 'The Trace of Levinas in Derrida', in *Derrida and Différance,* ed. David Wood and Robert Bernasconi (Evanston: Northwestern University Press, 1988), pp. 13–30.

28. I discuss Steerforth as Byronic in 'Illustrating Accusation: Blake's Illustrations to Dante', *Studies in Romanticism* 37 (1998), 395–421.

Part Three

Ecce Homo: Nietzsche

1

S HAKESPEARE AND DICKENS DRAMATISE a posthumous state. While being posthumous needs interpretation in *Cymbeline* and *David Copperfield*, Nietzsche already interprets the posthumous in conceptualising it. So does Benjamin. Though Nietzsche's and Benjamin's sense of the posthumous needs interpretation, in their turn they differ from Shakespeare and Dickens in degree of consciousness of the term's appropriateness to describe the relation between modernity and the past. In Nietzsche, narrative and metanarrative run side by side; especially in considering *Ecce Homo*, the text of the posthumous man, where autobiography and critique turn into each other.

However, a cluster of texts apply in considering Nietzsche and the posthumous, and we can start with the second edition of *The Gay Science* (1887). Nietzsche added a whole new book to the first edition of 1882, and this includes a section prefaced by the heading '*The hermit speaks*' (section 364). On 'the art of associating with people' is succeeded by '*The hermit speaks once more*' (section 365):

> But there are also other ways and tricks when it comes to associating with or passing among men – for example, as a ghost, which is altogether advisable if one wants to get rid of them quickly and make them afraid. Example: One reaches out for us but gets no hold of us. That is frightening. Or we enter through a closed door. Or after all lights have been extinguished. Or after we have died.

The last is the trick of *posthumous* people par excellence. ('What did you think?' one of them asked impatiently; 'would we feel like enduring the estrangement, the cold and quiet of the grave around us – this whole subterranean, concealed, mute, undiscovered solitude that among us is called life but might just as well be called death – if we did not know what will *become* of us, and that it is only after death that we shall enter *our* life and become alive, oh very much alive, we posthumous people!')[1]

So Nietzsche thought of himself as one of the posthumous people. Like Blake, who left this casual comment in a visitor's book, a year before his death:

William Blake, one who is very much delighted with being in good Company. Born 28 Novr 1757 in London & has died several times since. January 16 1826[2]

Blake, posthumous it seems (and admirer of Chatterton), taken as mad and neglected in his own lifetime – the beginning of the triumphalist nineteenth century – sorts well with Nietzsche. The aphoristic style of both Blake and Nietzsche assaults unitary statements, so that both risk being placed outside history by being misunderstood. Walter Kaufmann compares Nietzsche's refusal, as a posthumous person, of bourgeois society (newly unified Germany) with *The Gay Science*, section 262:

Sub specie aeterni. – 'You are moving away faster and faster from the living; soon they will strike your name from their rolls.' – B: 'That is the only way to participate in the privilege of the dead.' – A: 'What privilege?' – B: 'To die no more.'

In the last section of this added book, *The Gay Science*, section 382, 'The great health', Nietzsche associates others with him as 'new, nameless, hard to understand, we premature births of an as yet unproven future', and he demands for the 'new goal', a 'new health', 'the great health'. Posthumous people may also be premature births.

The Gay Science in its first edition had been succeeded by *Thus Spake Zarathustra*, and then by *Beyond Good and Evil* (1886), *The Genealogy of Morals* (1887) and *The Case of Wagner: A Musician's Problem* (1888). Including that last text, the year 1888 saw Nietzsche working on no less than *six* texts altogether, the others being *Twilight of the Idols, Nietzsche Contra Wagner,* the *Dithyrambs of*

Dionysus, and *The Antichrist*, which was to be subtitled 'Revaluation of all Values', but which he changed to 'A Curse on Christianity'. Then came *Ecce Homo*.

In the Preface to *The Antichrist* ('Revaluation of all Values') he comes back to the posthumous theme, which had first appeared in 1887:

> This book belongs to the very few. Perhaps not one of them is even living yet. Maybe they will be the readers who understand my *Zarathustra*: how *could* I mistake myself for one of those for whom there are ears even now? Only the day after tomorrow belongs to me. Some are born posthumously.[3]

2

After this declaration of the posthumous as the avant-garde, comes the truly posthumous text, *Ecce Homo*, the autobiography, which was to be virtually the last thing Nietzsche wrote. It included the chapter-title 'Why I Am So Wise':

> The good fortune of my existence, its uniqueness perhaps, lies in its fatality: I am, to express it in the form of a riddle, already dead as my father, while as my mother I am still living and becoming old.[4]

Nietzsche's father died at the age of thirty-six, in 1849. 'He was delicate, kind and morbid, as a being that is destined merely to pass by – more a gracious memory of life than life itself.' It was as if there was no father and no Oedipal conflict. But the death of the father is no cause for triumphalism; rather, 'already dead as my father', the son declares himself posthumous. David Copperfield was posthumous in that his father was already dead, but DC considers himself alive; Nietzsche, as all through his work, sees himself as posthumous, here specifically in the sense that *he* is dead when his father dies. The father embodies the past, being 'a gracious memory of life rather than life itself', but the son is not by that constituted as the present and alive. Instead, he writes the following, on the untitled page before 'Why I Am So Wise' It is the passage which serves as the exergue to *Ecce Homo*:

> On this perfect day . . . I looked back, I looked forward, and never
> saw so many and such good things at once. It was not for nothing
> that I buried my forty-fourth year today; I had the *right* to bury it;
> whatever was life in it has been saved, is immortal . . . *How could I
> fail to be grateful to my whole life?* – and so I tell my life to myself. (221)

He writes as though at the midday, the period of the shortest
shadow, which, as we shall see, is a moment of crisis. It is his
birthday (15 October 1888) – birthday of the long-dead Friedrich
Wilhelm, the king of Prussia for whom he was named, and always
a national holiday – and he calls it his burial-day. He looks *back*
to a state that is now gone; he is posthumous. He looks *forward*
to a posthumous existence, which is to be established in those
texts written and those still to be published. The posthumous
existence is not his own, and it is certainly not in his control
as the subject, which means that he can tell it to himself, but
not as the narrative of something that he has had the power to
bring about. In telling his life, he tells what is future to himself;
he thinks of the potentiality of his writings to give him an afterlife.

If he is dead as the father, so he has to give birth to himself
not as the decadent, as the father was, but as the figure of 'great
health', so becoming his mother. So 'as my mother' – creating
himself as the mother, as he is the mother of his books and
existing in the feminine – 'I live and grow old'.[5] The price is
high: 'I have almost paid with my life' he says – and he adds
that to understand *Zarathustra* the price is also high: 'one
must be similarly conditioned as I am – with one foot *beyond* life'
(226).

A subsequent chapter in *Ecce Homo*, 'Why I Write Such Good
Books', returns to the posthumous:

> I am one thing, my writings are another matter. – Before I discuss
> them one by one, let me touch on the question of their being under-
> stood or *not* understood. I'll do it as casually as decency permits, for
> the time for this question certainly hasn't come yet. The time for
> me hasn't come yet: some are born posthumously. (259)

What he is now and what he will be when he is known through
his writings are different, plural. That 'Nietzsche' – who is not
single, but the subject of endless interpretations – is to be born
posthumously. Is that an acceptance of the death of the author

as the single subject? Yes, but he is *already* dead; so there can be no single Nietzsche. As he says in *Ecce Homo*, discussing *Thus Spake Zarathustra*: 'One pays dearly for immortality: one has to die several times while being alive' (303). The immortal writer dies several times before his death; the writer who is merely of his time dies once, but fairly finally. Being posthumous saves him from being 'merely' fashionable, 'merely' of now: it is his privilege that he will die no more.

This 'posthumous' in Nietzsche may be compared with the title of the early text *Untimely Meditations* (*Unzeitgemässe Betrachtungen*). This has been variously translated: *Thoughts Out of Season, Untimely Considerations, Unmodern Observations, Unfashionable Observations, Unconventional Observations* or *Inopportune Speculations*.[6] What is *zeit-gemässe* is appropriate to the time, up to date, in fashion, or modern. What is untimely can never fit in with its time, it will never be opportune; if it is not modern, it may be postmodern. Or posthumous.

3

On 8 January 1889 Franz Overbeck came to Turin, where Nietzsche had been living since September 1888 (as he describes in the chapter on *Twilight of the Idols* in *Ecce Homo*). He found him working on the galley proofs of the *Dionysus Dithyrambs*, the last work that he sent to the press.[7] He took him back to Basel and then to Jena, and for the rest of his life, until 25 August 1900, Nietzsche was kept in care, in a state which may be called a virtual posthumous existence, possessed of Chatterton's 'noble insanity'; that is, diagnosed as suffering from a paralysis which had affected the brain, before he became truly posthumous. This meant that he never knew of the publication of his works of 1888.[8] We can probably discount the stories of a sudden collapse, and of embracing a horse being beaten in the streets of Turin, as a moment of crisis. The boundary between his activity in 1888, and the state of 'the absence of work', what Blanchot calls *désoeuvrement*, seems much more porous, and accelerated production seems to have come from an accelerated sense that his future would soon be one of worklessness, *désoeuvre-ment*.[9] Perhaps Nietzsche's perceptions of being posthumous include the premonition of his madness as a further form of the posthumous; but if so, the term 'the posthumous' questions the distinction between writing that belongs to philosophy and mad writing.

4

I shall return to *Ecce Homo*, but by a circuitous route that looks at Nietzsche and memory.

David Copperfield is caught by a present memory that he cannot shake off: the impossibility of forgetting and the melancholia this induces is the opening of 'The Uses and Disadvantages of History for Life', and as a preoccupation it runs through Nietzsche's work: the weight of a culture, a language and a tradition which inhibits the present; the gnawing power, like remorse, of always having to say 'It was', and the fear of identity as constructed by personal, and more than personal, history (Marx's 'weight of the dead generations, which lies like a nightmare on the brains of the living' – as *The Eighteenth Brumaire of Louis Bonaparte* puts it):

> for since we are the outcome of earlier generations, we are also the outcome of their aberrations, passions and errors, and indeed of their crimes; it is not possible wholly to free oneself from this chain. (76)

This point nearly brings to an end the third section of Nietzsche's 'The Uses and Disadvantages of History', and the issue of being caught by a paralysing memory and not being allowed to forget extends from there to the later texts, *Thus Spake Zarathustra* and *The Genealogy of Morals*. Nietzsche is preoccupied with a self-oppressive relation to history which can never be rationally legitimated, but which cannot be refused. Not to be able to forget, as regards personal history, implies that the subject is constructed by guilt-feelings, and it also means that a repressed and induced memory constructs the modern subject as the single subject. The third section of 'The Uses and Disadvantages of History' concludes with the passage already quoted, in relation to *David Copperfield* (see above, p. 64). There, the past may be re-interpreted – remembering that past events should not be read as one event leading to another (A causing B), but rather as one interpretation becoming victorious over another (B making A obsolete) – so that instead of history, Nietzsche proposes 'genealogy', working back from the present through distinctive levels of interpretation which the historian narrativises from the other direction.

History, as a study implying the need to copy and to follow given models, can only be justified 'for the future . . . as the attendant of a mighty new current of life, an evolving culture' (67). Nietzsche passes from discussion of three different approaches to history – the monumental, the antiquarian and the critical. The first allows the present to believe 'that the greatness that once existed was in any event once *possible* and may thus be possible again' (69), so it cuts out ideas of progress, being anti-Hegelian in allowing for the surprising, the out-of-time. Coming to the second approach, the antiquarian's piety towards the past serves life positively in that 'he wants to preserve for those who shall come after him the conditions under which he himself came into existence' (73), but the last approach, the critical permits forgetting, letting the past disappear (76). Turning, in the fourth section, to the newly unified Germany, Nietzsche comments on its possession by history, which does not permit it to go in its own direction; it is impossible for modernity to begin. In the opening of the fifth section, he refers to five respects in which 'the oversaturation of an age with history' (83) seems to him to be dangerous, and these respects are illuminated in the rest of the essay.

To summarise briefly: first, the personality develops a smattering of other forms of knowledge which do not match up with any personal growth of character, any self-stylisation, or possibility of self-fashioning. Then the modern age overrates its development in relation to the past; then, third, history 'disrupts the instincts of a people', preventing them from acting freely, making them, instead, become preoccupied with given models. It produces a devaluation of the present in relation to the past, and fifth, it leads to a cynicism and relativism which again paralyses. The conclusion is that 'history can be borne only by strong personalities' (86) – or, to put it in the terms of section six: 'he to whom a moment of the past *means nothing at all* is the proper man to describe it' (93); history is not for everyone, for most people are likely to be consumed by *ressentiment* in relation to it.

Being preoccupied with the past is to be caught up in something already interpreted; history-writing makes the past homogeneous and authoritative. Nietzsche ends section six with a discussion of biography, which is now, even more than in Nietzsche's time, the growth area in literary studies and the substitute for criticism. Biography promotes the origin of the work in the author as the single subject and as the superintending controlling consciousness in whom textual contradictions unite and its nostalgia gives the author a heritage status while placing him or her within a determinate history, which, however, he or she is, miraculously, master of and which may be understood, in terms of its motivations and psychosexual drives, in terms of the present having a continuity with it. As the opposite of the posthumous, then, Nietzsche advises against those biographies bearing 'the legend "Herr So-and-so and his age"' but is in favour of any Life subtitled 'a fighter against his age' (95). To read the writer cannot be to read the age, with which the writer does not fit. History must become awareness of the untimely, the heterogeneous within the apparently homogeneous; the awareness that the past cannot claim authority over the present because when it was a present itself, it was also oppressive; or, because containing forces heterogeneous to itself, it could never be said to be present.

5

In its first edition, *The Gay Science* culminated in section 340, referring to the dying Socrates, as the person for whom life was a disease, a figure of *ressentiment*, willing to be done with life, and in section 341, which raises the question of the 'eternal return'.

Socrates would not have willed eternal return: but how would the reader receive the idea of everything being repeated, and innumerable times more? Section 342, which concludes, begins '*Incipit tragoedia*' and leads into the opening of *Thus Spake Zarathustra*.

In the second edition of *The Gay Science*, with its added Book 5, section 382, 'The Great Health' shows the 'new spirit' demanding something new:

> [T]he ideal of a spirit who plays naively . . . for whom those supreme things that the people naturally accept as their value standards, signify danger, decay, debasement, or at least recreation, blindness and temporary self-oblivion; the ideal of a human, superhuman well-being and benevolence that will often appear *inhuman* – for example, when it confronts all earthly seriousness so far, all solemnity in gesture, word, tone, eye, morality, and task so far, as if it were their most incarnate and involuntary parody – and in spite of this, it is perhaps only with him that *great seriousness* really begins, that the real question mark is posed for the first time, that the destiny of the soul changes, the hand moves forward, the tragedy *begins*.

'The tragedy begins' loops back to the end of Book 4, section 342, '*Incipit tragoedia*'. The Preface to the second edition, however, makes this reference double. Nietzsche refers to the songs he has added, and says,:

> it is not only the poets . . . on whom the resurrected author has to vent his sarcasm; who knows what victim he is looking for, what monster of material for parody will soon attract him? *Incipit tragoedia* we read at the end of this awesomely awesome book. Beware! Something downright wicked and malicious is announced here: *incipit parodia*, no doubt. (33)

The words re-echo at the end of 'How the "True World" Finally Became a Fable' in *Twilight of the Idols*, which describe a moment which is 'post-histoire': 'Noon, moment of the briefest shadow; end of the longest error; high point of Humanity; INCIPIT ZARATHUSTRA' (486). In the moment of the briefest shadow, everything is at its flattest, and melancholia and boredom at its most intense, and the question is what can follow on? For Blanchot, the 'great Noon is the abyss of light from which we can never depart' – and he calls it nihilism, by which he means the impossibility of escaping from being, the impossibility of transforming it.[10] The answer is tragedy: Zarathustra going down. The answer is also parody.

Thomas Mann might have recollected these passages when in *Doctor Faustus*, Adrian Leverkühn, Mann's construction of Nietzsche, recalls a passage of music (probably the Prelude to Act 3 of *Der Meistersinger*), and after describing it, in a letter to Zeitblom, shows how he finds this 'serious' music devaluing itself: 'Dear friend, why do I have to laugh? . . . Why does almost everything seem to me like its own parody?'[11]

In Marx, 'the great events of world history occur . . . twice . . . the first time as tragedy, the second time as farce'. The 'invention of tradition' which accompanied the development of nation-states at the end of the nineteenth century, and whose latest form is the 'heritage' industry, means the imposition of inauthentic emotions, supposed to be a continuation of history, but actually parodic of it and of those historical emotions. The repetition of historical emotions in a present-day context, like dressing up in historical costumes, is likely to become parody, but the fear in *Doctor Faustus* relates to the sense that we have arrived at the 'end of art', to the end of texts being valued because they can be related to a linear history or tradition. *The Gay Science* notes, then, the importance of reading doubly, tragedy and parody combining, which also means the impossibility of reading being the activity of the single subject. The difference between 'The Uses and Disadvantages of History for Life' and the newer form of writing of *The Gay Science* is that in the earlier essay, the past was reinvented to protect present identity, but this identity is more in question now. The new spirit, inhuman, posthumous, because it has a doubled space of existence, moves against inscriptions of the subject as single. Nor can 'the great seriousness' become solemnity, which would always feed the thought of how deep, how profound the bourgeois subject really is.

6

Incipit Zarathustra – and everything in *Thus Spake Zarathustra* – counters a narrative that defines the present subject as the product of the past, which will also define the future. The section 'Redemption' (Book 2, section 20) defines revenge as the will's 'antipathy to time and its "it was"' (recalling a similar passage in 'The Uses and Disadvantages of History', see above pp. 64, 97). It is followed with a passage opposing the will's frustration as it reflects that time is not in its power:

> Verily, a great folly dwells in our will; and it has become a curse for everything human that this folly has acquired spirit.
>
> *The spirit of revenge,* my friends, has so far been the subject of man's best reflections; and where there was suffering, one wanted punishment too.
>
> For 'punishment' is what revenge calls itself; with a hypocritical lie it creates a good conscience for itself.
>
> Because there is suffering in those who will, inasmuch as they cannot will backwards, willing itself and all life were supposed to be – a punishment. And now cloud upon cloud rolled over the spirit, until eventually madness preached, 'Everything passes away; therefore everything deserves to pass away. And this too is justice, this law of time that it must devour its children.' Thus preached madness.
>
> Things are ordered morally according to justice and punishment. Alas, where is redemption from the flux of things and from the punishment called existence? Thus preached madness.
>
> 'Can there be redemption if there is eternal justice? Alas, the stone *It was* cannot be moved: all punishments must be eternal too.' Thus preached madness.
>
> 'No deed can be annihilated: how could it be undone by punishment? This, this is what is eternal in the punishment called existence, that existence must eternally become deed and guilt again. Unless the will should at last redeem itself, and willing should become not willing.' But, my brothers, you know this fable of madness.
>
> I led you away from these fables when I taught you, 'The will is a creator'. All 'it was' is a fragment, a riddle, a dreadful accident – until the creative will says to it, 'But thus I willed it'. Until the creative will says to it, 'But thus I will it, thus shall I will it.'[12]

When 'it was' looms in the consciousness as like a great stone that cannot be shifted, it generates a belief in the present as

99

suffering, which will be followed by punishment, or in past suffering being replaced by present punishment. It relates to a narrative where events are causally connected. 'It was' sets the agenda. The present and hence the future become mere consequences of the past. The past as that which cannot be laid to rest remains the father, like the melancholic Saturn who destroys the present by eating his children; just as the present, father of the future, destroys the future in its turn. And the present devours the past, too: it is also part of this attitude that the past is 'punished' by being emptied of significance.

As it is not possible to alter the past, no 'punishment' in the present or future can ever suffice, so the future too must be contaminated, and must continue to pay for the present, as the present pays for the past. The only way out of that is a further devaluation of existence, which says that we ought to deny the will to live – which is Schopenhauer's pessimism.

In this section, as in the discussion of history in the *Untimely Meditations*, Nietzsche assumes that the person who can look back, who can use history, can only do so out of a complete and contented relationship to the present: 'if you are to venture to interpret the past, you can only do so out of the fullest exertion of the vigour of the present' (*Untimely Meditations*, 94). A narrowed and alienated present cuts off the ability to read the past, or leads to its overvaluation or to its idealisation; or perhaps the construction of *ressentiment* as the dominant within bourgeois modernity means that the past cannot be read, except in kitsch or parodic form, so depriving the present of the uses of history. The route Nietzsche's text takes, however, is not to contest that present, but to change modes of thinking of how the subject who is constructed by *ressentiment* can become other. The redemption from this *ressentiment* against life, which founds all other *ressentiments*, is by 'thus I willed it', which instead of seeing the past as dominant, makes it something that can be shaped by the present, reinterpreted. When this is said, a narrative re-creating the past becomes one creating the future and implies as a consequence another possibility which, as in *The Gay Science*, needs to be affirmed: eternal return.

7

When eternal return reappears as a thought in the *Thus Spake Zarathustra* ('The Vision and the Riddle', Book 3, section 2), for the dwarf it is a further way of suggesting the powerlessness of the will: if time does go round in a circle, then everything will always be repeated identically. What has been must recur just as it was before.

But the argument that imposes repetition as a structural necessity also dissolves the category of the subject – events recur ceaselessly, but events create the subject who appears at the end of them. X does not repeat his actions. Eternal return, which assumes that the 'same' person repeats the 'same' actions, is also parodic (I will return to this point), since it dissolves the idea of sameness (and so cannot exist as a discrete doctrine: it is the doctrine which dissolves doctrines). We cannot stand outside the circle of return, and say that the person at the end of the second action is the same person who was at the beginning of the first or the second action. (Nor are these two beginnings the same: the second time the 'repeated' action is performed, it would be by and on a subject constructed through the previous action.) It is an abstraction to say that the subject-state at the end of an action is the same as it was at the beginning. To start from the end of an action, as the point from which to read, which licenses saying that a person repeats his actions, constructs events like a detective novelist – working from subsequent effects to prior causes, which, once they have been intuited or constructed, are written as causes followed by effects, as in the way the reader follows the detective novel. Reading forwards gives the appearance of a logical sequence, but the thing has been put together, as in historical interpretation, from the end backwards.

Posthumous existence begins with eternal return, whose implications make history not that of the single subject who is bound to a single reading of time. Nietzsche's posthumous subject has a discontinuous existence, where to be dead or to be alive are not opposites. *Ecce Homo*, to return now to that text, says 'behold the man', but the man does not appear, for 'some are born posthumously'. 'How One Becomes What One Is' as subtitle does not allow for a determinate subject when the subject created is textual, formed through the pages of *Ecce Homo*. Further, *Ecce Homo*, after the Foreword and the Exergue, and after such chapters as 'Why I Am So Wise', 'Why I Write Such Excellent Books', with titles which make the book a parody of a *Bildungsroman*, turns into a substantial eleven chapters named for and discussing the writing of the 'excellent books', books whose impact, it is said, is yet to be felt, yet in the future, yet to be born, implying the ongoing power of textuality. How one becomes what one is, is through writing books, *and* through writing *Ecce Homo*, which both supplements the books and is a book in itself, suggesting that the self will never be wholly formed, since the logic would be to add a further chapter called '*Ecce Homo*' to another book . . . and so on with that future book, and for ever after.

Identity is always deferred then, as it must always be the subject of deferral, as in a passage in 'Why I Am So Clever'. In this section, qualities are not to be named, for to name them would be to misname them. The passage asks for non-interpretation by the consciousness – which is 'a surface' – and therefore unaware of the sources of what it tries to interpret:

> To become what one is, one must not have the faintest notion *what* one is. From this point of view even the *blunders* of life have their own meaning and value – the occasional side roads, the delays, 'modesties', seriousness wasted on tasks that are remote from *the* task. All this can express a great prudence, even the supreme prudence: where *nosce te ipsum* [know thyself] would be the recipe for ruin, forgetting oneself, *misunderstanding* oneself, making oneself smaller, narrower, become reason itself. (254)

After speaking in this 'how to' mode, the text turns to give auto-biography:

> An order of rank among these capacities; distance; the art of separating without setting one against one another; to mix nothing, to 'reconcile' nothing; a tremendous variety that is nevertheless the opposite of chaos – this was the precondition, the long, secret work and artistry of my instinct. Its *higher protection* manifested itself to such a high degree that I never even suspected what was growing in me – and one day all my capacities, suddenly ripe, *leaped forward* in their ultimate perfection . . . At this very moment I still look upon my future – an *ample* future – as upon calm seas: there is no

ripple of desire. I do not want in the least that anything should become different than it is; I myself do not want to become different. (254–5)

It becomes evident that this self-fashioning is 'an attempt to give oneself . . . a past in which one would like to originate in opposition to that in which one did originate' (*Untimely Meditations*, 76). The writing deliberately refuses to note the unconscious of its remarks. It makes no confession, refusing that mode, but treats the 'instinct' in a wholly innocent manner as something that could not be known ('I never even suspected') – because what could know the instincts? Only a patriarchal force, which has the power to name and to bring into recognition, and extort confession, and the father, a synecdoche for patriarchal history, has died. The writing disavows desire, including sexual desire, yet, in thinking about an ample future, has not given up on desire. Desire must be unacknowledged because that would also imply, as an opposite, the power of abjection, hatred of the body and bodily desire, and as he says, '*nausea* at man is my danger' (331). How to become what one is? The answer is by fictionalising the self, to the extent of making the subject of writing a parody, refusing the reality-principle.

Nietzsche's indeterminateness is, self-consciously, brought to a climax in the last chapter, 'Why I Am A Destiny', which starts:

> I know my fate. One day my name will be associated with the memory of something tremendous – a crisis without equal on earth, the most profound collision of conscience, a decision that was conjured up *against* everything that had been believed, demanded, hallowed so far. I am no man, I am dynamite. (326)

This passage thinks of a date in the future which will be post-crisis, when Nietzsche's name is associated with an event which will have brought about a change, such as the one Foucault outlines at the end of *The Order of Things*, where 'man' is seen as

> an invention of recent date. And one perhaps nearing its end. If those arrangements [of language and of discourse] were to disappear as they appeared, if some event of which we can at the moment do no more than sense the possibility – without knowing either what its form will be or what it promises – were to cause them to crumble,

as the ground of Classical thought did, at the end of the eighteenth century, then one can certainly wager that man would be erased, like a face drawn in sand at the edge of the sea.[13]

With this post-man epoch occurring after the end of history, and entailing the removal of the abstract, ungendered universal 'man' as a product of that history and as a template organising thought and action, there will be, Nietzsche thinks, a period of looking back which will invest his name with significance, not as the name of the cause that moved the change, but a reminder that Nietzsche serves as an image for that future state. At that stage, people will be ready to read Nietzsche. This would be the posthumous creation of 'Nietzsche' as, in Benjamin's terms, to be explored in Part Four, a 'fact becoming historical posthumously'. Becoming historical means becoming 'Nietzsche', however endlessly interpreted. As Kaufmann points out at this point in a footnote, Nietzsche takes up a statement quoted in a review about his work in 1886, that he was not a man, but dynamite, and reapplies it. In the future (not yet) he will become what he is *now* – i.e. in the 1880s, at the time of writing, an event, an impersonal shaping force, like dynamite, derived from the very Greek word for power. When will he exist? Now (1888) when he is not yet alive (but posthumous) or then when his work is ready to be read (the day after tomorrow) when his existence will be established as a founding *différance*, a force which splits the rock? Either way, this writing is performative, creating a difference, writing that will be seen as constructing history, so that the 'day after tomorrow' will have to work with a model of history that allows it to think of 'Nietzsche' and to let that name influence it.

But it is not a simple day after tomorrow, for this writing takes place under the shadow of the eternal return. What 'Nietzsche' will be in the future has been there in the past, which means that the Nietzschean potential is available at all moments: not just Nietzsche after Hegel; but Nietzsche before Hegel, for instance – 'it is always before and after Hegel that Nietzsche comes and comes again'[14] – just as in *Ecco Homo* (283) Nietzsche recalls that he dedicated the first edition of *Human, All Too Human* 'to the memory of Voltaire, in commemoration of his death, May 30 1878', as if suggesting that Nietzsche and Voltaire are contemporaries (in Voltaire's posthumous existence) and that Voltaire enables a reading of Nietzsche, and Nietzsche a reading of Voltaire.

8

Existence in Nietzsche is not that of the single subject, but of an irreducible multiplicity of impulses and drives.[15] The Preface to *Ecce Homo* says, 'Hear me! for I am such and such a person' (217). *Ecce Homo* breaks off with 'Have I been understood?' – *Dionysus versus the Crucified* – (335) which makes 'what one is' double, or contradictory, the split between two gods and impelled towards both. There can be no separation between either. The first is twice-born (taken from Semele as she died, so posthumous in relation to his mother and reborn from the thigh of Zeus). And if God is dead, then the Crucified must also have been posthumous. Dionysus against the Crucified expresses antagonism against the negation of life (life as suffering, the impulses and drives needing to be punished), and the incompleteness of the sentence suggests that this is how the future will be: contestation between these two.

Kaufmann's note to the passage refers to the collection of fragments which Nietzsche's sister collected and called *The Will to Power*, and to section 1052, written earlier in 1888. The fragment suggests that Dionysus represents 'life itself', which includes torment and destruction. 'In the other case, suffering – the "Crucified as the innocent one" – counts as an objection to this life . . . – One will see that the problem is that of the meaning of suffering, whether a Christian meaning or a tragic meaning . . . Dionysus cut to pieces is a *promise* of life: it will be eternally reborn and return again from destruction.'[16]

Being cut to pieces, going down, as was happening while Nietzsche was writing 'Why I Am a Destiny', is how one becomes what one is. The body in pieces has no identity. At the same time, in letters to Peter Gast and Georg Brandes (both 4 January 1889) Nietzsche signs himself as 'The Crucified', so that he is indeed both gods. On 5 January 1889, he writes to Jacob Burkhardt from

105

Turin, assuming a posthumous identity, since God is dead, or a series of identities:

> Dear Professor, when it comes right down to it, I'd much rather have been a Basel Professor than God; but I didn't dare be selfish enough to forgo the creation of the world. You see, one must make sacrifices, no matter how and where one lives. – But I did secure a small room, fit for a student, opposite the Palazzo Carignano (in which I was born as Victor Emmanuel) from whose desk I'm able to hear that splendid music coming from below me, in the Galleria Subalpina. I pay 25 frs. including service, make my own tea and do all my own shopping, suffer from torn boots, and constantly thank heaven for the *old* world, whose inhabitants weren't simple and quiet enough.
>
> Since I am doomed to entertain the next eternity with bad jokes, I'm busy writing, which leaves nothing to be desired, is very nice and not at all taxing. The post office is five steps away; I take the letters in myself, handing the great *feuilletoniste* over to high society. Naturally I'm on intimate terms with *Figaro*. And so that you'll have an idea of how harmless I can be, here are my first two bad jokes:
>
> Don't take the case of Prado too seriously. I am Prado, I'm also Prado's father, and I venture to say that I'm Lesseps too. I wanted to give my Parisians, whom I love, a new concept – that of a decent criminal. I'm Chambige too – also a decent criminal.
>
> *Second joke*. I salute the Immortals. Monsieur Daudet belongs to the Forty.
>
> Astu
>
> What's unpleasant and a strain on my modesty is that in fact I am every historical personage; and as for the children I've brought into the world, I ponder with some misgiving the possibility that not everyone who enters the 'kingdom of God' also comes *from* God. This fall, dressed as scantily as possible, I twice attended my funeral, the first time as Count Robilant (– no, he's my son, in so far as I'm Carlo Alberto in my nature here below), but I was Antonelli myself. Dear Professor, you ought really to see this edifice. Since I'm quite inexperienced in the things I'm creating, you have a right to make any criticism; I'll be grateful, but can't promise that I'll profit from it. We artists are incorrigible.
>
> Today I looked at an operetta (ingeniously Moorish) and took the occasion to ascertain, with joy, that now both Moscow and Rome are grandiose affairs. You see, my talent for landscape is undeniable as well. – Think it over; we'll have a really fine chat, Turin isn't far, no serious professional obligations tie us down, a glass of Veltliner could easily be procured. Informal dress is *de rigeur*.
>
> With heartfelt love. Your
>
> Nietzsche

> I go everywhere in my student coat, now and then slap someone on the back and say, *siamo contenti? son dio, ho fatto questa caricatura.*
>
> Today my son Umberto is coming here with lovely Margherita, but I'll receive her as well only in shirtsleeves.
>
> The *rest* is for Frau Cosima – Ariadne – From time to time we practise magic.
>
> I've had Caiaphas put in chains; I too was crucified last year in a long, drawn-out way by German doctors. Wilhelm Bismarck and all anti-Semites done away with!
>
> You may make any use of this letter which will not lower me in the esteem of the people of Basel.[17]

The dead God identifies both with Vittorio Emanuele, who had died in 1878, and with dead criminals. He has twice attended his own funeral, first as Count Robilant, 'the most admirable example of Piedmontese nobility, the natural son . . . of King Carlo Alberto' – so Nietzsche writes in a letter to Overbeck of 13 November 1888 – and now he claims to be the father of Robilant, while also claiming to be Antonelli, the Papal secretary of state under Pius IX. It is a posthumous existence, to have survived two funerals, the continuation of speaking of his birthday as burying his forty-fourth year.

This letter moves through a series of masks (personae): the trivial gossip-columnist, as the man at ease; as the man whose transgressiveness flouts dress proprieties because he knows that there is no 'proper' identity, because he makes the rules. The persona identifies with criminals, just as *Ecce Homo*, discussing Shakespeare (seen as a mask for Bacon in another emptying out of identities), says that 'the strength required for the vision of the most powerful reality is not only compatible with the most powerful strength for action, for monstrous action, for crime – it presupposes it' (246). In another identity, the figure is Dionysus, soliciting Cosima Wagner as Ariadne after she has been doubly 'deserted' by Wagner (in his death, and, in his life, by writing bourgeois music); and he is also the Crucified, as he recalls Caiaphas, and the German doctors (i.e. instruments of normality) and the power of national anti-semitism. If there is one sense to be taken from this it is of competing and unignorable intensities operating upon him, as and because the subject has in his turn surrendered the sense of a single identity. Instead, he is 'every historical personage'.

That statement, claiming to be every name in history, Deleuze and Guattari, influenced by Pierre Klossowski,[18] take to mean not an identification with specific personages, but with effects: with the force-fields that these names embody.[19] These intensities, or states, or force-fields, Nietzsche identifies with the names of people in history, such as Dionysus and the Crucified. Belief in eternal return puts to an end any belief in present single identity – let alone an identity which could recur. Fascism has been the name of the cultural politics – and nationalist politics – that has premised itself on belief in single identity, and denial of the other; Klossowki's Nietzsche is outside fascism though aware of it. Belief that identity covers contrary force-fields, unless under the force of a repression which keeps these out by labelling them as evil, produces a Deleuzian schizophrenia. The difficulty in acknowledging multiplicity when the subject is forced into a single-subject condition, under the power of Caiaphas, or the doctors, or the anti-semites, different agencies of surveillance, produces a breakdown – an alternative form of passive schizophrenia – a posthumous state which may be understood psychically, independent of whatever might be said about the physical causes of Nietzsche's breakdown.

According to Klossowski, in *Nietzsche and the Vicious Circle*, the eternal return of the same, which asserts that 'in the beginning was the return' as Blanchot, who also follows Klossowski, puts it,[20] cannot allow for the assumption of single identity, or its resumption. As the idea of eternal return means that there is no first time or origin in history, and no end of history, it entails also the end of a history premised upon linked events, so that if we define history as 'the work', since in it everything is significant, then the doctrine of eternal return means worklessness (the state where there is no single controlling ego), or complete 'l'absence d'oeuvre' – madness.[21]

If in *Ecce Homo*, discussing the *Untimely Meditations*, Nietzsche says that the essays on Wagner and Schopenhauer 'speak only of me' (281), that cannot privilege Nietzsche above these two, for it rather means that the present subject, with the task of being in the present, continues what these earlier names represent. If the same could return in the cycle of eternal recurrence, that would necessitate accepting the identity of the same at the present moment; but identity cannot be so established. It is simulacral, a copy, in the specialised sense in which Klossowski uses the term. Where Klossowski speaks of a 'phantasm', he means 'an obsessional image produced instinctively from the life of the impulses', while a simulacrum 'is a willed reproduction of a phantasm that simulates his invisible agitation'.[22] Thus each *name* of history becomes an image for Nietzsche, and each *identity*, including his own, no more than a parody of the idea of a true, unique identity. That is where modernity has got to: it imposes as an ideology the single subject, and it gets that in parodic form again. Wagner, in contrast to Nietzsche, was histrionic, because 'he used the simulacrum while remaining *totally unconscious* of the false' (Klossowski, 223). This is why Wagnerian music 'turns into its own parody'. Since it believes in its unique self, it must assert its own single being too insistently, which makes it often solemn, and at the same time, a subject for laughter. And the doctrine of eternal return is, as said before, parodic of a 'true' doctrine, insofar as its existence as a doctrine allows for the same identity, yet its conditions disallow the possibility of the 'true', which is replaced by a multitude of simulacra.

As Blanchot puts it, commenting on Klossowski on Nietzsche:

> [T]he image ceases to be second in relation to the model . . . imposture lays claim to truth . . . finally there is no longer an original but an eternal scintillation in which the absence of origin, in the blaze of the detour and return, disperses itself.[23]

Eternal return allows for the return of all possible intensities, which are felt as possible at one moment. They are re-willed, as is clear from *Thus Spake Zarathustra*, but they cannot be re-willed as mine, for, as Klossowski says, 'this possessive no longer has any meaning, nor does it represent a goal' (Klossowski, 70). Willing the eternal return wills therefore the disappearance of the subject, and there is a connection between willing that and Nietzsche's madness. Both are taking the subject out of history; eternal return is a mode of ceasing from the madness that the end of history and the 'post-histoire' state implies. While the eternal return may be the source of laughter and of joy, it also means that the weight of intensities falls upon the historical Nietzsche, which for all his posthumous existence, an existence which took him out of Oedipal structures and out of a relation to history he was not able to bear, he was also not able to live with; hence the madness, which has, therefore, at least two separate and irreconcilable explanations, first as the product of his awareness that all existences come together in him as possibilities, and the second familiar explanation, the brain paralysis.[24]

Blanchot comments on Klossowski on Nietzsche, in the fragmentary writing of *The Step Not Beyond*. The writing of Blanchot's book refuses a system, because a system would have to be grasped in the present; instead it 'risks a thought no longer guaranteed by unity' (*The Infinite Conversation*, 153), so allowing for contradictoriness. *The Step Not Beyond* argues that if the present cannot be established, if it is lack, since the 'same' has no place to which it can return, this has implications for both past and present. It 'mak[es] us live as in a state of perpetual death'.[25] The 'present' seemed linked to 'presence', as a linear conception of time promotes the present and presence, which would include the idea of the subject being self-present to itself, having a single and present identity. But now past and present become de-realised, no longer working within a chronology. Each present moment becomes, instead, a gap, a caesura – to say which recalls the births of Macduff and of Posthumus, both of whom were ripped out of a sequence of events. 'I cannot delve him to the root', as the First Gentleman says of Posthumus, because there is, despite the history he gives, no past, no origin, to account for the present Posthumus. The 'caesura' is Hölderlin's term for the impossible event which makes past and future no longer fit, no longer rhyme – which as an impossible present makes all being posthumous.[26] As Deleuze writes:

> The caesura . . . must be determined in the image of a unique and tremendous event, an act which is adequate to time as a whole. This image itself is divided, torn into two unequal parts. Nevertheless, it thereby draws together the totality of time . . . [but] . . . as unequal parts. Such a symbol . . . may be expressed in many ways: to throw time out of joint, to make the sun explode, to throw oneself into the volcano, to kill God or the father. This symbolic image constitutes the totality of time to the extent that it draws together the caesura, the before and the after.[27]

It seems that as Zarathustra accepts the doctrine of the eternal return of the same, so too Nietzsche's writing can do no other than turn more and more towards a writing of the fragment which, as Blanchot puts it, 'does not depend on the present' (*The Step Not Beyond*, 55). It is not even offered for understanding, as an utterance about which a decision could be made. Nietzsche's adoption of eternal return takes him away from a usual form of existence – that of being chained to history, and caught in a logic of identity; it impels him instead towards a life of writing where the self is constituted in writing whose existence is also posthumous in relation to the event.

Notes

1. *The Gay Science*, trans. Walter Kaufmann (New York: Vintage Books, 1974), p. 321.
2. William Blake, Inscription in the Autograph Album of William Upcott, *Complete Writings*, ed. Geoffrey Keynes (Oxford: Oxford University Press, 1966), p. 781. Blake's subsequent death was in 1827.
3. *The Portable Nietzsche*, edited and translated by Walter Kaufmann (Harmondsworth: Penguin, 1976), p. 568.
4. Nietzsche, *The Genealogy of Morals and Ecce Homo*, trans. Walter Kaufmann (New York: Vintage, 1989), p. 222.
5. For a discussion of the implications of this riddle, see David Farrell Krell, *Infectious Nietzsche* (Bloomington: University of Indiana Press, 1995), pp. 213–33. Krell compares the readings of Gasché, Derrida, Sarah Kofman and Pierre Klossowski, and quotes Nietzsche's revised chapter 'Why I Am So Wise' which was suppressed by his mother and his sister, and only brought to light in 1969, and which most clearly indicates Nietzsche's hostility to his mother and sister: both of them aspects of the 'all too human' he rejected, and, in the case of the sister, fiercely anti-semitic.
6. See *Untimely Observations*, trans. R. J. Hollingdale, introduction by Daniel Breazeale (Cambridge: Cambridge University Press, 1997), pp. xliv–xlvii. The Ernst Behler

edition, based on that of Giorgio Colli and Mazzino Montinari (Stanford: Stanford University Press, 1995), vol. 2, trans. Richard T. Gray, translates *Unzeitgemässe Betrachtungen* by 'Unfashionable Observations' (see pp. 395–9 for discussion) while it also translates the second essay of the book as 'The Utility and Liability of History for Life'. 'Skirmishes of an Untimely Man' is one of the titles appearing in *Twilight of the Idols.*

7. See Thomas Harrison, 'Have I Been Understood? The Eternal Nowhere of Nietzschean Existence', *Stanford Italian Review* 6 (1986), p. 182.

8. *The Antichrist* and *Nietzsche Contra Wagner*, appeared in 1895; *Ecce Homo* in 1908; other Nietzschean texts were assembled as *The Will to Power* in 1901.

9. Foucault's definition of madness as the 'absence of work' comes from the Preface to his *Folie et Déraison: Histoire de la Folie à l'Age Classique* (Paris: Librarie Plon, 1961), p. v; the passage does not appear in the English translation, *Madness and Civilization*: it implies the absence of anything productive that society would recognise; the absence of anything that can be used.

10. Maurice Blanchot, 'Reflections on Nihilism', in *The Infinte Conversation*, trans. Susan Hanson (Minneapolis: University of Minnesota Press, 1993), p. 149.

11. Thomas Mann, *Doctor Faustus*, trans. H. T. Lowe-Porter (Harmondsworth: Penguin, 1968), p. 131.

12. Translation of *Thus Spake Zarathustra* from *The Portable Nietzsche*, pp. 252–3.

13. Michel Foucault, *The Order of Things*, trans. Alan Sheridan (London: Tavistock, 1970), pp. 386, 387.

14. Blanchot, *The Step Not Beyond*, trans. Lycette Nelson (Albany: State University of New York, 1992), p. 22.

15. See Christoph Cox, 'The "Subject" of Nietzsche's Perspectivism', *Journal of the History of Philosophy* 35 (1997), 93–115.

16. Nietzsche, *The Will to Power*, trans. Walter Kaufmann (New York: Vintage Books, 1967), pp. 542–3.

17. Nietzsche, letter to Jakob Burkhardt, 5 January 1889, in *Nietzsche: A Self-Portait from his Letters*, trans. Peter Fuss and

Henry Shapiro (Cambridge, MA: Harvard University Press, 1971), pp. 142–4. See also the translation in Kaufmann, pp. 685–7.

18. Pierre Klossowski, *Nietzsche and the Vicious Circle*, trans. Daniel W. Smith (Chicago: University of Chicago Press, 1997). On Klossowski, see Gilles Deleuze, in *The Logic of Sense*, trans. Mark Lester with Charles Stivale, and edited by Constantin V. Boundas (London: Athlone Press, 1990), pp. 280–301. 'Klossowski's entire work moves towards a single goal: to assure the loss of personal identity and to dissolve the self' (p. 283).

19. Deleuze and Guattari, *Anti-Oedipus*, p. 86.

20. Maurice Blanchot, 'The Laughter of the Gods', in *Friendship*, trans. Elizabeth Rottenberg (Stanford: University of Stanford Press, 1997), p. 181.

21. I take this point from Vincent Descombes, *Modern French Philosophy*, trans. L. Scott-Fox and J. M. Harding (Cambridge: Cambridge University Press, 1980), p. 112.

22. Translator's note, p. xi of *Nietzsche and the Vicious Circle*.

23. Maurice Blanchot, 'The Laughter of the Gods', in *Friendship*, p. 180.

24. A third explanation for this most posthumous state, not developed here, appears in Nietzsche's 'Significance of Madness in the History of Morality', *Daybreak* section 14; where 'all superior men who were irresistibly drawn to throw off the yoke of any kind of morality and to frame new laws had, *if they were not actually mad*, no alternative but to make themselves, or pretend to be mad' – trans. R. J. Hollingdale, ed. Maudmarie Clark and Brian Lester (Cambridge: Cambridge University Press, 1997), p. 14.

25. Maurice Blanchot, *The Step Not Beyond*, trans. Lycette Nelson (Albany: State University of New York, 1992), pp. 12, 55.

26. See Philippe Lacoue-Labarthe, 'The Caesura of the Speculative', in *Typography: Mimesis, Philosophy, Politics* (Stanford: Stanford University Press, 1998), pp. 208–35; this quotes (p. 234) from Hölderlin: 'For the tragic *transport* is properly empty and the most unbound. Whereby, in the rhythmic succession of representations, in which the *transport* presents itself, *what in metre is called the caesura*, the pure word, the

counter-rhythmic intrusion, becomes necessary in order to meet the racing alternations of representations at its culmination, such that what appears then is no longer the alternation of representations, but representation itself.' (An alternative translation of this passage appears below, p. 148.)

27. Gilles Deleuze, *Difference and Repetition*, trans. Paul Patton (London: Athlone Press, 1994), p. 89.

Part Four

'Posthumous Shock': Walter Benjamin's History

1

I N THE WINTER OF 1939/40, Walter Benjamin, freed from an internment camp at Vernuche, worked in Paris, at the Bibliothèque Nationale, on the 'Arcades' project, which had occupied him throughout the 1930s, and writing the theses 'On the Concept of History', *Über den Begriff der Geschichte* (translated as 'Theses on the Philosophy of History'). Benjamin refers to that title in thesis 10, when he comments on 'the high price our accustomed thinking will have to pay for a conception of history that avoids any complicity with the thinking to which these politicians [those who have become complicit with fascism] continue to adhere'.[1] In May 1940, he left Paris as it fell to the Nazis, and ended by taking his life at Portbou on the Spanish border, on 26 September 1940.[2] On leaving Paris, Benjamin left his papers with Georges Bataille, including the *Angelus Novus* picture by Paul Klee, and his work has continued to appear posthumously.

The 'Theses on the Philosophy of History' – the last thing Benjamin wrote, and first published in full ten years later – ends with a section 18, which then has two following sections, called A and B, the first focusing on the historian, the second on the soothsayer. In section A:

Historicism contents itself with establishing a causal connection between various moments in history. But no fact that is a cause is

115

for that reason historical. It *became historical posthumously*, as it were, through events that may be separated from it by thousands of years. A historian who takes this as his point of departure stops telling the sequence of events like the beads of a rosary. Instead he grasps the constellation which his own era has formed with a definite earlier one. Thus he establishes a conception of the present as the 'time of the now' which is shot through with chips of Messianic time. (265, my emphasis)

Discovery of the posthumous here becomes a 'point of departure' for beginning to think about the past and history, and how the past becomes historical. Benjamin's argument is interventionist, implicitly assuming a first-person position, because it is aimed at the 'historian' who must change his practice of history-writing. The target he aims at is historicism, first identified as a mode of thinking at the end of the First World War in Germany. Historicism gives history as a narrative, conceptualising it in terms of cause and effect, as a chain of events, as neutral time, which is marked out flatly, in the mode that cartography measures space. Into that history, everything must be fitted, and understood on the basis of its relation to it. On this interlocked basis, everything in the past is read as of equal importance or unimportance – as in the aestheticism or fetishism implied in 'telling the sequence of events like the beads of a rosary'.

Yet rendering history as a narrative conceals something else. In 1899, Freud published 'Screen Memories', which begins with the proposition that 'it is only from the sixth or seventh year onwards – in many cases only after the tenth year – that our lives can be reproduced in memory as a connected chain of events'.[3] The 'chain of events', implying that narrative replaces something else that is inaccessible, is a phrase taken over by Benjamin. But we have seen it also in Nietzsche, in *The Genealogy of Morals* (II.xii), when he speaks not of a chain of events but of a 'chain of signs'; and just as Nietzsche's thinking here anticipates the Saussurian image of language as a metonymic displacement from signifier to signifier, where language is 'a system of differences without positive terms', a 'chain of signs' not only abolishes the distinction between the event and its semiotic representation, but pulls both into a continuing reinterpretation where the event is the way it has been represented. This does

not abolish the facts, though it recognises that a fact is inseparable from its semiotic value, but it asks how linking fact to fact
in a chain of events is inseparable from the mobilisation of signs,
so that the first chain (events) cannot be thought without the
second (signs).

The ending of Freud's essay is relevant:

> It may indeed be questioned whether we have any memories at all
> *from* our childhood: memories *relating to* our childhood may be all
> that we possess. Our childhood memories show us our earliest years
> not as they were but as they appeared at the later periods when the
> memories were aroused. In those periods of arousal, the childhood
> memories did not *emerge*, they were *formed* at that time. (322)

The narrative by the subject to the subject of a 'chain of events'
screens out other memories. The argument of Benjamin turns
on the comparison with historical narration. To narrate is to
presume on things being taken as cause and effects. But a fact
becomes historical 'posthumously', not by being inserted into a
narrative or being fundamental to one. The past is formed in
the present, posthumously. It comes into discourse analeptically,
in relation to a present, and since it is read from the standpoint
of the present, its being is proleptic as well in that it forms 'the
time of the now' (*Jetztzeit*). The 'chip' at work in it Derrida calls
the 'shard, splinter, *Splitter*, that the messianic inscribes in the
body of the present'.[4]

2

'On the Concept of History' is a collection of fragments, or snap-
shots, but it contains several arguments, including one which
begins with 'the state of emergency' in which Benjamin found
himself in the winter of 1939/40 in Paris, and with the knowledge that this state of emergency is – for some – no more than
normal oppression. The target then is the threatened triumph
of fascism, and Benjamin writes that 'one reason why Fascism
has a chance is that in the name of progress its opponents treat
it as an historical norm' (viii.259). 'Progress' reappears in several
following theses.

The first, famously, is attached to the figure of the angel of history, a passage which has to be imagined in three forms. First, the absent Paul Klee picture *Angelus Novus*, which must be read, as an image in an emblem book demands, allegorically. Then, like a seventeenth-century emblem book, with the Gershom Scholem verses printed under the emblem, and then as an *impresa* which unfolds the ambiguities within the image. In the seventeenth-century emblem books, three different forms – the image, the couplet and the *impresa* – made for discontinuities and a lack of single attributable meaning in the allegorical emblem. So it is here. I quote from the *impresa* to this fragmented emblem:

> His face is turned toward the past. Where we perceive a chain of events, he sees one single catastrophe which keeps piling wreckage upon wreckage and hurls it in front of his feet. The angel would like to stay, awaken the dead, and make whole what has been smashed. But a storm is blowing from Paradise; it has got caught in his wings with such violence that the angel can no longer close them. This storm irresistibly propels him into the future to which his back is turned, while the pile of debris before him grows skyward. This storm is what we call progress. (ix.259–60)

The angel looks back at what has not been healed, what remains 'untimely, sorrowful, unsuccessful'. The character of these things – fragmented, ruins – makes irrelevant historicist talk of a 'chain of events' or a 'continuum' (xiv.263, xv.263) or a 'sequence of events' (xviiiA.265), all of which are read here as the assumption of 'homogeneous, empty time' (xiii.263, xiv.263, xvii.264, 265, xviiiB.266). Nietzsche, in the eternal return had implicitly destroyed causality; Benjamin's point is rather to show how much ideology subtends belief in a chain of events. The angel can see, but the angel is dumb, in a state of shock, and the wind that blows from the Paradise that was the place of origin but which ejected humanity prevents him from going back to that past; instead he is propelled into the future. The storm, which disallows an attention to the catastrophic, is progress.

What the angel can see is what we cannot. We see progress, he sees catastrophe; but catastrophe need not be taken as the end of everything. Rather, 'the concept of progress should be grounded in the idea of catastrophe. That things "just go on" *is* the catastrophe'.[5] Apocalypse and continuity are not opposites; just as the events of the death camps continue their effects – as Blanchot observed – in a numbing, pervasive and banal manner. Progress may also be called catastrophe, which means that the angel sees the same things as 'we' do, but he reads them as an allegorist, where the appearances of unity and of development (the ideology of progress relates also to the ideology of the symbol) resolve into fragments, ruins, which mount skyward. In the sixteenth century, Dürer pictured melancholia as an angel in an allegory, surrounded by 'the utensils of active life . . . lying around unused on the floor' (*The Origins of German Tragic Drama*, 140); placed in no relation to each other. Benjamin now describes the allegory of the allegory; the angel breaks down what is seen into fragments or wreckage, which is the allegorical act, removing the signs of connectedness, which the idealism of historicism produces.

But the image of the angel requires allegorical reading in its turn, for it is not simply a matter of what the angel sees. Shocked, unable to move, unable to speak, posthumous in being severed from the past to which he is turned, he would like to 'awaken the dead and make whole that which is smashed': as if the past could be amended. He has the melancholy of the allegorist but also, more dangerously, the nostalgic melancholy of the figure who would like to reverse everything of the defeats of the past. The storm from Paradise propels him, against his will, into the future. But Paradise, while it is in the past, is also in the future; for, as Benjamin quotes Kraus in thesis xiv, 'origin is the goal'.[6] The angel's back is turned towards the future, and 'this storm is what we call progress' – as apocalyse and progress are the same in our present state – so 'progress' misnames, rationalises, the storm. All is ambiguous within this 'dialectical image': the androgyny of the angel; the two forms of vision; the split forms of melancholy; the ambiguity of the storm; the double location of Paradise, and the ambiguity which this creates as to which is the past and which is the present.

3

The doubleness of the meaning of 'progress' disallows the theses from being taken as a narrative; but in the next section, Benjamin comments on the politicians who have made common cause with fascism – for their 'stubborn faith in progress, their confidence in their "mass basis", and . . . their servile integration in an uncontrollable apparatus have been three aspects of the same thing' (x.260). The third of these topics is explicated in section xi, which rounds on German Social Democracy's interest in 'technological developments'. 'Progress' appears a sentence later; and then Benjamin refers to the new enslavement of a class of workers to such factory production (the conditions of German 1920s *Neue Sachlichkeit*). 'It recognises only the progress in the mastery of nature; not the regression of society; it already displays the technocratic features later encountered in Fascism' (xi.261). The attack on fascism as expressed in the Epilogue to 'The Work of Art in the Age of Mechanical Reproduction' is recalled. Fascism aestheticises politics through the gratifications of technology.

> Progress as pictured in the minds of Social Democrats was, first of all, the progress of mankind itself (and not just advances in men's ability and knowledge). Secondly, it was something boundless, in keeping with the infinite perfectibility of mankind. Thirdly, progress was regarded as irresistible . . . The concept of the historical progress of mankind cannot be sundered from the concept of its progression through a homogeneous, empty time. A critique of the concept of such a progression must be the basis of any criticism of the concept of progress itself. (xiii.262–3)

Progress depends on a concept of time as homogeneous and empty; but for Benjamin, history is not that, but 'time filled with the presence of the now' (*Jetztzeit*). The translator adds in a note that the quotation marks are there to differentiate the term from *Gegenwart* – the present. The 'now' is immanent in every moment of history, so that Robespierre can think of 'ancient Rome' as a 'past charged with the time of the now which he blasted out of the continuum of history'. Robespierre did not identify the present with the past, he saw the past as containing the energies of the present, and to do that, to lay hold of that dynamic, he destroyed the continuum, which is almost to say that he destroyed the concept of history, in denying the pastness of the past.

Robespierre's advantage was that such a representation of the past as not being different from the present could still work. The Revolution preceded the ideology of historicism, which, as an early nineteenth-century construction, succeeded. Perhaps Marx is more aware of that, and of the folly of appearing to go back, and so the passage can be seen as Benjamin contra the Marx of *The Eighteenth Brumaire of Louis Bonaparte*. For whereas Marx saw the return to models of Rome in the bourgeois revolution of 1789 as a regression, a sign of timidity and of the control of the past, which would pull the present back into its own simpler formulations (and unable to help since they were concerned with simpler moments), Benjamin reads it as a quotation, just as 'fashion [which has 'a flair for the topical'] evokes costumes of the past' (xiv.263). Fashion demonstrates the opposite of what, going by its connection with the notion of being 'modern', would be expected. 'Modern' has to do with 'today': 'modo' means 'recently'. But fashion does not pursue a single chronological development; it regards everything as potentially citable. (But since only a redeemed humanity can find everything of its history citable, it would also have to be said that fashion tolerates a total form of alienation, complete separation from knowing the content of its form.) Finding a moment in the past 'topical', it defines the time of the now not as 'now' meaning the present, but rather as bringing about the present. 'Now' is a performative, in which ancient Rome may be a part; the concept of the 'now' virtually abolishes the past as past (except as the past of the present).

Discussing urban experience, Benjamin uses notions of 'shock', with plural senses (the angel is in shock). The passage has bearings on thesis xiv:

> Of the countless movements of switching, inserting, pressing and the like, the 'snapping' of the photographer has had the greatest consequence. A touch of the finger now sufficed to fix an event for an unlimited period of time. The camera gave the moment a *posthumous shock*, as it were. Tactile experiences of this kind were joined by optic ones . . . moving through this traffic involves the individual

in a series of shocks and collisions. At dangerous crossings, nervous impulses flow through him in rapid succession, like the energy from a battery. Baudelaire speaks of a man who plunges into a crowd as into a reservoir of nervous energy.[7]

The flash of light from the camera links shock with electricity, and recalls the phrase 'charged with the time of the now'. Urban space is a field of force, defined in terms of electric charges: moving through the city is akin to moving through past and present; going through a field saturated with energy. In such a space, illumination comes as a flash, like the experience Baudelaire describes in 'A Une Passante' in *Les Fleurs du Mal*. Robespierre, by making something akin to fashion's 'tiger's leap into the past' (when the tiger leaps, it does not miss its target; fashion knows what to go for in the past), set up a new tradition, and Benjamin implies that tradition and fashion are inseparable. Fashion may be unerring in its target, but whether it has been successful – or fashionable: in other words, whether it has become what it is – can only be known later, through its success in foreseeing the present.[8] Yet that 'later' is not later; it is now, it is present. Fashion must create tradition, otherwise tradition becomes 'conformism' (vi.257) – which is a point for T. S. Eliot in 'Tradition and the Individual Talent'. When tradition is not conformism, it generates fashion.

4

In this force-field of writing, there is also the presence of Nietzsche. His essay, 'On the Uses and Disadvantages of History for Life' (1874), has its foreword quoted: 'we need history, but not in the way a spoiled loafer in the garden of knowledge needs it'(vi.262). Another Nietzschean passage is relevant:

> *Historia abscondita.*[9] – Every great human being exerts a retroactive force: for his sake all of history is placed in the balance again, and a thousand secrets of the past crawl out of their hiding places – into *his* sunshine. There is no way of telling what may yet become part of history. Perhaps the past is still essentially undiscovered! So many retroactive forces are needed! (*The Gay Science* section 34)

The notion of the 'retroactive' has already appeared in an earlier Benjaminian thesis, which begins with the class struggle, and emphasises that the victors in that 'have retroactive force and will constantly call in question every victory, past and present, of the rulers' (iv.257). The new victors would be Nietzsche's great human beings. It is easy to link this with the way an event 'became historical posthumously'. A retroactive force creates the posthumous – where the 'fact' is changed into something historical, by which it gains the power of an image.

5

The ideology of progress creates a dangerous determinism; the moment must be 'blasted' out of the continuum or the continuum 'exploded' (xv.263, xvi.264), to free a space in which to rethink time. Benjamin compares the calendar and the clock. One marks time in terms of memory, recalling it, and overlaying one moment upon another, creating an unconscious for each date it singles out, and implying that there was a collective mentality which he calls a 'historical consciousness', which he says has not been apparent in Europe for the last hundred years. This, taken literally, means that historical consciousness was lost somewhere around 1840, i.e. at the time of the triumph of nineteenth-century 'history' and of bourgeois taste, about the time of *David Copperfield*. The other, technologically adept, gives time running emptily onwards, and now, in the case of digitalised clocks, not even allowing to each moment a before and after. Benjamin compares the initial day of a calendar to 'a time-lapse camera' – a camera recording an event over a period of time, like a flower unfolding. The time-lapse camera, bringing the event and chronological time into a new relationship, pluralises time, makes it contain something else. Elsewhere, Benjamin uses the comparable image of a fan;[10] folded and unfolded, the fan implies both the moment, and its potentialities – which make time not homogeneous and empty. Historicism, in contrast, as it appears in section xvi, fixes the past in the past.

In writing on Baudelaire's title 'Spleen et idéal' from *Les Fleurs du Mal,* Benjamin links these two concepts with the dominance of the clock over the calendar. 'The *idéal* supplies the power of remembrance; the *spleen* musters the multitude of the seconds against it.' While the *idéal* remembers, and so is linked to the Proustian notion of *mémoire involontaire,* which we may call a form of the posthumous, the *spleen* (anger, melancholia) results from the 'inability to experience' that Benjamin diagnoses as being 'at the heart of rage'. Benjamin links this to the misanthropy of Timon of Athens, and quotes Barbey d'Aurevilly calling Baudelaire a Timon-figure. Timon's hatred is directed against the cynicism with which the instrumental rationality of modernity works – moving from one sensation to another but with nothing taking hold in the consciousness.[11] It is, effectively, rage directed at what is entailed in 'homogeneous, empty time', which is a cynical construction, a mode of killing each moment in the moment of its passing. *Timon of Athens* does not depend upon the sexual, or a determinate cause such as the threat of imperialism to motivate its anger and melancholia: in this way it is different from *Cymbeline.* Yet significantly, Timon, in Shakespeare's play, modern in its anticipation of this, can make no impact on Athens save in a posthumous state, making himself an emblematic figure in letting the sea wash over his grave, and leaving an epitaph to be read after death; for him, 'My long sickness / Of health and living now begins to mend / And nothing brings me all things' (*Timon of Athens,* V, i, 185–7). It is not so much a question whether there is life after death, as – taking the graffiti Paul Virilio reported seeing in Belfast, 'Is there is life before death?'[12] 'The outbreaks of rage are linked to the ticking of the seconds to which the melancholy man is slave.' Clock time, progress, modern existence as the deprivation of experience – these things are sources of deep anger against the ideology of progress, whose motivations may be defined in terms of the refusal to allow experience to take hold. For progress, while it seems to uphold the presence of the present, demands the supercession of the present moment.

Et le Temps m'engloutit minute par minute,
Comme la neige immense un corps pris de roideur.[13]

So opens the last section of Baudelaire's poem desiring oblivion, and asking in the last line for total oblivion, like Timon covered by the waves, 'Avalanche, veux-tu m'emporter dans ta chute?' – Avalanche, will you take me in your fall? The avalanche is the weight of events. This anger is directed against time piling up and covering over past possibilities of experience. The image associates with the angel of history, who can do nothing about the wreckage that, piling up, is inseparable from the ideology of progress, which has created it, and which now makes it impossible to give attention to it.

Benjamin continues the Baudelairean reference, however, by saying that 'though chronology places regularity above permanence, it cannot prevent heterogeneous, conspicious fragments from remaining within it'. These are, of course, what a *mémoire involontaire* would have a recognition of:

> To have combined recognition of a quality with the measurement of the quantity was the work of the calendars in which the places of recollection are left blank, as it were, in the form of holidays. The man who loses his capacity for experiencing feels as though he is dropped from the calendar. (*Baudelaire*, 144)

The calendar allows for experience; the clock disallows it, so that the clock effectively disallows history. Robespierre disallowed the past in refusing to accept its pastness, but the nineteenth-century compensated for the disallowing of history in relation to experience which the discipline of history meant, through the orthodoxy of historicism. I now turn to this topic.

6

Benjamin makes sport with historicism in thesis xvi, seeing it as like a bordello that sends away its male customers exhausted; they have been enticed into giving all their energy into an enjoyment of the past as the past. That accords with the definition historicism received beforehand:

> To historians who wish to relive an era, Fustel de Coulanges recommends that they blot out everything they know about the later course

of history. There is no better way of characterising the method with which historical materialism has broken. It is a process of empathy whose origin is the indolence of the heart, *acedia*, which despairs of grasping and holding the genuine historical image as it flares up briefly. Among medieval theologians it was regarded as the root cause of sadness . . . The nature of this sadness stands out more clearly if one asks with whom the adherents of historicism actually empathise. The answer is inevitable: with the victor. And all rulers are the heirs of those who conquered before them. Hence, empathy with the victor invariably benefits the rulers. (vii.258)

Historicism is here taken as a laziness which fails to re-read and so thinks in terms of linear development – progress – rather than in terms of Nietzschean genealogy. The reference to history being the history of the rulers, and so of new, triumphal interpretations being overlaid on top of each other, each the interpretations of successive victors, echoes Nietzsche's *The Genealogy of Morals* (II.xii). Historicism buries itself in a period, relives an era, finding that easier than grasping 'the historical image'. The historicist does not reason that history can only exist in representation – 'the past can be seized only as an image' – not as a narrative, and, as an image, an emblematic one, 'which flashes up at the instant when it can be recognised, and is not seen again' just as 'every image of the past which is not recognised by the present as one of its concerns threatens to disappear irretrievably' (v.257).

The historicist's melancholia contrasts with and is also similar to that of the melancholic angel, remembering that, as I argued above in my section 2, the melancholic historicist is also nostalgic. Becoming nostalgic is the opposite of becoming posthumous, because it creates a simulacrum of the past, rather than giving the past an afterlife. The laziness takes the form of 'empathy', which is the belief that it is possible to identify with the other, to enter into his or her world. In practical terms, empathy shows its emptiness since it always sides with the victors; in other words, it identifies with those whose story has become the preferred one. Empathy denies the pastness of the past, it abolishes difference, and can only exist at all on the basis of a preferential view of what is past (belief in the immediacy of Shakespeare, for instance). The belief in empathy thus refuses to read the present. And since the historicist tells us not to consider the later, subsequent stages of history, this does mean an implicit devaluation of the present. A chiasmic structure emerges. Historicism devalues the *present*, while as the narrative of progress it devalues the *past* in favour of the present. But it also devalues the present because it is only interested in securing the future; but it is not interested in the future either, since Benjamin contends that mankind's 'self-alienation has reached such a degree that it can experience its own destruction as an aesthetic pleasure of the first order' ('The Work of Art in the Age of Mechanical Reproduction', *Illuminations*, 244). The passage recalls the warning implicit in the end of *The Genealogy of Morals*: 'man would rather will nothingness than not will'.

Reading the present gives urgency to seeking out a moment in history which can appear in a citable form. To articulate the past historically means 'to seize hold of a memory as it flashes up at a moment of danger. Historical materialism wishes to retain that image of the past which unexpectedly appears to man singled out by history [the historical subject] at a moment of danger' (vi.257). The memory, which is an image of the past, comes unexpectedly, as *mémoire involontaire*, about which Benjamin quotes Proust saying that 'it was a matter of chance' if it could work at all (*Baudelaire*, 113). To make the past speak, to make it citable, requires being in the present and yet being also distant from it. If it speaks, that is 'hope in the past'.

Stopping the clocks, the image of section xv, returns in xvi, where the historical materialist needs a present where 'time stands still and has come to a stop', and in xvii, where 'thinking involves not only the flow of thoughts, but their arrest as well. When thinking suddenly stops in a configuration present with tensions, it gives that configuration a shock, by which it is crystallised into a monad' (xvii.264–5). Thinking, the allegorist's activity, comes across a 'configuration' which is a 'Messianic cessation of happening'. The word 'configuration' compares with the word 'constellation' in xviiiA, where the historian 'grasps the constellation which his own era has formed with a definite earlier one'. At such a moment, when the past is established in its image-force as something 'historical' posthumously, 'he establishes a conception of the present as the "time of the now" which is shot through with chips of Messianic time'.

7

The historian who tells the sequence of events like the beads of a rosary is in a different mode from the 'chronicler who recites events without distinguishing between major and minor ones', working on the basis that nothing should be lost for history. But 'only for a redeemed mankind has its past become citable in all its moments' (iii.256) – citable since nothing is now repressed, or silenced. An event may be citable in the sense that it can be referred to, or in the sense that it can now be quoted, which means that it now works in the present. Like fashion, a statement becomes a quotation by being cited; that is its posthumous existence. When Benjamin says that the French Revolution saw itself as 'the return of Rome' (this is modifying Zohn's translation 'Rome incarnate'), the return is that of the repressed, traumatic return, in a form of *Nachträglichkeit*. Here, quoting is not simply voluntaristic, assuming something from the past (not the same as *The Eighteenth Brumaire*). Rather, it is a means whereby the present finds itself changed, and not through its own agency. Benjamin writes 'quotations in my work are like armed highway robbers who loom up and relieve the idler of his convictions'.[14] Quotation is a manifestation of the *mémoire involuntaire*, and, linked with the historical image, it implies that what comes back of the past is an image – not an image *of* the past, but an image *in* the present which reaches back to the charged moment. All depends in Benjamin's thinking, on this crossover, which negates past/present distinctions: the present gives everything to the past, turning a past fact into something historical. At the same time, the past gives everything to the present.

Saying 'the past carries with it a temporal index by which it is referred to redemption. Our coming was expected on earth. Like every generation that preceded us, we have been endowed with a *weak* Messianic power, a power to which the past has claim' (ii.256), Benjamin gives weight to what has been 'untimely' and 'unsuccessful' in history. But, to make a comparison, the sense of incompleteness is apparent even in such a triumphal text as Walt Whitman's 'Crossing Brooklyn Ferry' (though it was unsuccessful, and attacked, when it was written, in the 1850s). Whitman thinks of others who will be crossing years hence:

> It avails not, time nor place – distance avails not,
> I am with you, you men and women of a generation, or ever so many
>   generations hence.
> Just as you feel when you look on the river and sky, so I felt
> Just as any of you is one of a living crowd, I was one of a crowd.
>   (20–3)[15]

This from *Leaves of Grass*, in crossing Brooklyn ferry crosses generations, and assumes the poet's then present death ('I felt', not 'I feel'). He assumes something more complete in being posthumous, and having a readership yet to come, which created by his poetry, will have made it become, posthumously.

In 'The Task of the Translator', Benjamin says that 'no poem is intended for the reader, no picture for the beholder, no symphony for the listener' (*Illuminations*, 69). This reflects upon meditations being always 'untimely', and denies a punctual relationship between text and reception; just as it also makes the work imageless, not corresponding to its age, or giving an image of it – where an image would allow for the assumption that reality can be read in a mode that can be captured imagistically.

8

The image is the subject when Benjamin speaks of the arresting of a flow of thoughts in 'a configuration pregnant with tensions' (again the force-field image), and the shock-effect of that is that the configuration crystallises into a monad. In 'A Short History of Photography', Benjamin says that it is through photography 'with its devices of slow motion and enlargement . . . that we first discover the existence of [the] optical unconscious' (*One Way Street*, 243). The photograph, by its interruption, arresting a flow, brings about 'the dialectic at a standstill' (*Baudelaire*, 171). Later, Benjamin finds the same optical unconscious in cinema's close-ups, montage and slow-motion photography:

Our taverns and our metropolitan streets, our offices and furnished rooms, our railroad stations and our factories appeared to have us locked up hopelessly. Then came the film and burst this prison-world asunder by the dynamite of a tenth of a second, so that now, in the midst of its far-flung ruins and debris, we calmly and adventurously go travelling. ('The Work of Art', *Illuminations*, 238)

Cinema performs the work of allegory, turning the 'prison' in a moment into the ruin, and pluralising vision. The spatial images used here pair with the time-images of the 'Theses', for it is evident that homogeneous, empty time – the prison – which is blasted out of existence, exists spatially too, and to find 'unconscious optics' (*Illuminations*, 239) in the cinema may be read as the opening up of a temporal gap in viewing. The discovery readmits, as Miriam Hansen puts it, 'dimensions of temporality and historicity . . . a disjunction that may trigger recollection, and with it, promises of reciprocity and intersubjectivity'.[16] The uncertainties *David Copperfield* displays about what value to attribute to anything within the text, Benjamin would see as highlighted by the optical unconscious of the photograph and the film, working like psychoanalysis which is the link between nineteenth-century modes of perception and twentieth. It is as if the nineteenth century needed psychoanalysis to explain both its novels and it, psychoanalysis, as with the 'Dora' fragment, or the Wolf-man, becoming a form of novel-writing, and as if the twentieth century tested psychoanalysis as a possibility through film.

The language of 'the camera [giving] the moment a posthumous shock', which I quoted earlier, is an image of dialectical ambiguity. The camera renders the moment dead; it associates with the clock which kills each second in turn. In William Faulkner's *The Sound and the Fury*, on the day of his suicide, Quentin Compson wakes and thinks:

and then I was in time again, hearing the watch. It was Grandfather's, and when Father gave it to me, he said, 'Quentin, I give you the mausoleum of all hope and desire'.[17]

The statement is a declaration of *ressentiment* against time and its 'it was'. Coming from the culture of the 'Lost Cause' of the Southern States, Mr Compson declares history – which is, here, a selective history of white tradition – to be over before anything happens; it denies the posthumous because it cannot bear to read the past. Faulkner aligns clock-time with patriarchy; as though, like Saturn, both of them embodied the power of the past to kill each second as it arrived. The photograph has an ambivalent relationship to that. It complies with it, yet it also makes each moment that was killed – that it killed to make it live again as an image – alive again in a posthumous space, out of the dominion of a patriarchal ideology of past/present/future. To live posthumously seems to be to live without patriarchy – including the patriarchy of the self – in an unauthorised existence such as that of the photograph. Since the photograph creates everything as posthumous, posthumous images become the mode of perception of modern culture, making a dream of immediacy cease, and giving to perception the sense that everything exists in a posthumous state.

In the notes deriving from the 'Arcades' project which were to be used for the 'Theses', Benjamin writes:

> Where thought comes to a standstill in a constellation saturated with tensions, there appears the dialectical image. It is the caesura in the movement of thought. Its positioning, of course, is in no way arbitary. In a word, it is to be sought at the point where the tension between the dialectical oppositions is the greatest. The dialectical image [. . .] is identical to the historical object; it justifies blasting the latter out of the continuum of history's course.[18]

The 'standstill', which recalls Posthumus's repeated word 'stand, stand' in *Cymbeline*, is the caesura, too, and this articulates with Posthumus's caesarian birth. What emerges is not the reconstitution of the past as a narrative, but the discovery of an image, which itself is tense with past and present and future moments. The posthumous shock gives in the image a concentrate which is both spatial, and of time. This as a caesura in the movement of thought, which happens at every moment, indicates that all thinking must be as images that do not connect as continuous narrative, which, as caesural breaks even the movement of narrative, and it brings together Shakespeare, Nietzsche, Benjamin and Deleuze.

9

One last take on Benjamin and the image. Gilles Deleuze's two books on cinema show the influence of Walter Benjamin's readings; they are part of Benjamin's afterlife. In *Cinema 1* and *Cinema 2* (1983, 1985), Deleuze registers a break between the cinema of the 'movement-image' and that of the 'time-image'. He hints at the difference between the two in this provocative example, which seems like an instance of posthumous shock:

> Now, suppose a character finds himself in a situation, however ordinary or extraordinary, that's beyond all possible action, or to which he can't react. It's too powerful, or too painful, or too beautiful. The sensory-motor link's broken. He's no longer in sensory-motor situation, but in a purely optical and aural situation. There's a new type of image.[19]

The cinema of the movement-image, even though it should not be periodised strictly, Deleuze links with pre-1939 cinema. Showing the passage of time through movement, its interest in time is indirect, and the quotation above associates it with a sense of the subject's autonomy. In the time-image, the subject of cinema turns to time, and with the paralysis or traumatic state described above, we could compare the state of shock of the angel of history. Deleuze says that this new situation 'allows us to catch or reveal something intolerable, unbearable, even in the most everyday things' (*Negotiations*, 51). And again, that fits with the angel of history. The cinema of the time-image does not reduce time to a function of space by thinking of the present as a model for consideration of past and future. Rather, it thinks of space as disconnected and empty, 'any space whatever', so that time rises to the surface of the screen.

Discussing the time-image, Deleuze resists the idea that cinema gives an image of the present. 'What is specific to the image . . . is to make perceptible, to make visible, relationships of time which cannot be seen in the represented object and do not allow themselves to be reduced to the present.'[20] The image is not that of something existing at a single point in a single identity; Deleuze draws from Bergson the notion of 'continuous multiplicities' which the duration of time brings out.[21]

Later, Deleuze quotes Godard:

It is characteristic of cinema to seize this past and this future that coexist with the present image. To film what is *before* and what is *after* . . . Perhaps it is necessary to make what is before and after the film pass inside it in order to get out of the chain of presents. For example, the characters: Godard says that it is necessary to know what they were before being placed in the picture, and will be after. 'That is what the cinema is, the present never exists there, save in bad films'. (*Cinema* 2, 37–8)

A moment later, Deleuze adds that 'the direct time-image always gives us access to that Proustian dimension where people and things occupy a space in time which is incommensurable with the one they have in space'.

This meditation on the cinema and the time-image extends Benjamin on the photograph and its power of the 'optical unconscious' and its freeing of the moment from 'homogeneous, empty time', lighting up the moment like a flash with a sense of multiplicity and difference. Deleuze's use of Bergson is like Benjamin's: Deleuze summarises Bergson saying:

[T]he only subjectivity is time, non-chronological time . . . and it is we who are internal to time, not the other way round. That we are in time looks like a commonplace . . . Time is not the interior in us, but just the opposite, the interiority in which we are, in which we move, live and change . . . In the novel it is Proust who says that time is not internal to us, but that we are internal to time, which divides itself in two, which loses itself and discovers itself in itself, which makes the present pass and the past be preserved. (*Cinema* 2, 82)

The 'time-image' places the subject within a time which cannot be narrated, where narration would assume a true account, which is moving from a known past towards a present. By doing so it destroys the thought of the origin. In relation to this, Deleuze refers to 'the powers of the false', so that the cinema of the time-image has 'freed itself of appearances as well as truth: neither true nor false, an undecidable alternative' (*Cinema* 2, 145), just as the narrative in it

ceases to be truthful, that is, to claim to be true, and becomes fundamentally falsifying. . . . Crystalline description was already reaching the indiscernability of the real and the imaginary, but the falsifying narration which corresponds to it goes a step further and poses inexplicable differences to the present and alternatives which are undecidable between true and false to the past. (*Cinema* 2, 131)

In the 'crystal image', the real and the virtual co-exist (crystallise), so that 'the actual is cut off from its motor linkages, and the virtual . . . from its actualisations' (*Cinema 2*, 126–7). In the time-image, what is real, and what is imaginary, is indiscernible, and for this idea of the substitution of the 'power of the false' for 'the form of the true', which is at the heart of modern cinema, Deleuze cites Nietzsche.

The return of the same, after all, in Nietzschean terms, would mean the return of the false, since there is no single identity, nor single present moment that can return. What returns in posthumous form (whether neo- or retro-, or recycled or reconstituted) is always different, unfathered by the past, but its effect is, nonetheless, that history can never again be equated just with the category of what happened in the past. For these neo-forms are not necessarily activated by the past: instead, they create it; the new forms in the present are what posthumously constitute the past.

Notes

1. Benjamin, *Illuminations*, trans. Harry Zohn (London: Jonathan Cape, 1970), p. 260. I refer in the text to each thesis by number and page.
2. See Momme Brodersen, *Walter Benjamin: A Biography*, trans. Malcolm R. Green and Ingrida Ligers, ed. Martina Dervis (London: Verso, 1996), pp. 244–62.
3. Freud, 'Screen Memories', in *Standard Edition* 3 (London: Hogarth Press, 1962), p. 303. I take the reference from Siegfried Wenzel, *Body- and Image-Space: Re-reading Walter Benjamin* (London: Routledge, 1996), p. 59.
4. Jacques Derrida, *Spectres of Marx: The State of the Debt, The Work of Mourning and the New International*, trans. Peggy Kamuf (London: Routledge, 1994), p. 181.
5. Walter Benjamin, 'Central Park', trans. Lloyd Spencer, *New German Critique* 34 (1985), p. 50

6. On this, see Gershom Scholem, 'Walter Benjamin and his Angel', in *On Walter Benjamin: Critical Essays and Recollections*, ed. Gary Smith (Cambridge, MA: MIT Press, 1988), pp. 51–89.

7. Walter Benjamin, *Charles Baudelaire: A Lyric Poet in an Age of High Capitalism*, trans. Harry Zohn (London: Verso, 1973), p. 132, my emphasis.

8. Benjamin writes 'we always perceive past events "too late" and "politics" needs the "presence of mind" to "foresee" the present' – quoted, Susan Buck-Morss, *The Dialectics of Seeing: Walter Benjamin and the Arcades Project* (Cambridge, MA: MIT Press, 1989), p. 442.

9. Kaufmann annotates this as 'concealed, secret, or unknown history'.

10. Walter Benjamin, *One Way Street and Other Writings*, trans. Edmund Jephcott and Kingsley Shorter (London: Verso, 1979), p. 75.

11. See my 'Hating Man in *Timon of Athens*', *Essays in Criticism* 50 (2000), 145–68.

12. Paul Virilio / Sylvere Lotringer, *Pure War*, trans. Mark Polizotti (New York: Semiotext(e), 1983), p. 140.

13. The Baudelaire poem is no. LXXXII of *Les Fleurs du Mal*: 'Le Goût de Néant'. 'And minute by minute Time engulfs me, as the snow's measureless fall covers a motionless body'. Quoted, *Baudelaire*, p. 143; discussion pp. 142–4.

14. Quoted, Irving Wohlfarth, 'On the Messianic Structure of Walter Benjamin's Last Reflections', *Glyph* 3 (1978), pp. 148–212.

15. Walt Whitman, *Leaves of Grass*, ed. Sculley Bradley and Harold W. Blodgett (New York: W. W. Norton, 1973), p. 160.

16. See Miriam Hansen, 'Benjamin, Cinema and Experience: "The Blue Flower in the Land of Technology"', *New German Critique* 40 (1987), 217.

17. William Faulkner, *The Sound and the Fury* (Harmondsworth: Penguin, 1964), p. 73.

18. Quoted, Susan Buck-Morss, p. 219.

19. Gilles Deleuze, *Negotiations 1972–1990*, trans. Martin Joughin (New York: Columbia University Press, 1995), p. 51.

20. Gilles Deleuze, *Cinema 2: The Time-Image*, trans. Hugh

Tomlinson and Robert Galeta (London: Athlone Press, 1989), p. xii. (*Cinema 1: The Movement-Image,* 1986.)

21. On this, see Paul Douglass, 'Deleuze's Bergson: Bergson Redux', in Frederick Burwick and Paul Douglass, *The Crisis in Modernism: Bergson and the Vitalist Controversy* (Cambridge: Cambridge University Press, 1992), p. 375. The quotation is from Deleuze's *Bergsonism* (1966; trans. Hugh Tomlinson and Barbara Habberjam; New York: Zone Books, 1988), p. 39.

Afterlife

Ghostly Fathers / Unfathered Vapours

1

IN *FUTURES PAST*, THE historian Reinhardt Koselleck speaks of the first use, in 1870, of the word *Neuzeit*, as meaning new time, modernity, one of whose implications is that in its use, 'history was temporalized'. A new emphasis on time makes that the motor-force within history, while

> *Neuzeit* lent the whole of the past a world-historical quality. With this, the novelty of a history in emergence, assumed a progressively growing claim to the whole of history. It became regarded as self-evident that history as world-history had to be continually re-written.[1]

Modernity, which now becomes a way of relegating things to specific periods in the past, making the past clearly definable in contrast to a present, places events further and further back in 'the past' to make that clearly differentiated, just as a stress on linearity in the study of history does; but such a separation between past and present is crossed by the presence of a ghost.

Shakespeare and Dickens both show, amply, the unappeased nature of ghosts. Nietzsche thought that posthumous people should be among other people like ghosts. Ghosts are reminders of the power of the posthumous, their challenge in the present moment being whether the present is powerful enough to recognise their existence. As the uncanny, ghosts question, through the Freudian definitions of the *unheimlich*, whether the present can claim difference from the past, or whether it exists in repetition – as the Nietzschean 'dwarf' thinks in 'The Vision and the

Riddle'. The narrative of the past they give, however, is also questioned by the Freudian meaning of the uncanny, in that the past is also shown to lack the power of an origin.

In the film *Rouge* (1987), directed by the Hong Kong director Stanley Kwan, ghosts, reminders of the power of the posthumous, have many implications for the present as also posthumous. The heroine, Fleur (Anita Mui), is seen both in 1930s Hong Kong, as the inmate of a brothel (these scenes also contain a sideways look at then contemporary Shanghai culture – a city whose being then doubled that of Hong Kong), and as a ghost in the 1980s, looking for her lover, Chan Chen-pang (Leslie Cheung). He survived the lovers' double suicide pact in the 1930s, and Fleur is now looking for him.[2] The urban landscape of Hong Kong in the 1930s is now unrecognisable; functions have altered, but the modernised city is full of the ghosts of past buildings. Perhaps the insight is similar to that of Baudelaire, who noted how 'le spectre en plein jour raccroche le passant' ('the ghost in plain day greets the passer-by' – see 'Les Sept Vieillards', in *Les Fleurs du Mal*). Urban space is ghostly space: the aggressively modern city, by tearing down what is classed as of the past before it has a chance to be old creates the ghostly as a possibility. But equally, the present city threatens to make all perception ghostly, in that it removes the possibility of relationship with its architectural shapes, and deprives the senses through its creation of a certain intangibility within urban space. So Baudrillard, who speaks of the urban environment as deathly, claims that

> [O]ur true necropolises are the computer banks or the foyers, blank spaces from which all human noise has been expunged, glass coffins where the world's sterilised memories are frozen.

Baudrillard quotes the passage in Benjamin already cited (p. 127) on how humanity has become so self-alienated (under the influence of fascism with its control of technology and its aestheticising of politics) that it has reached the stage that 'it can experience its own destruction as an aesethetic pleasure'. Baudrillard applies this to the spectacle in which everything exists within the modern city.[3] Here, the designer-label has become the art-object, showing how the commodity has become the spectacle, thus mystifying its origins and character as it is counted as art; the system, Baudrillard writes, 'doubles itself as signs'. The ghost, however, exists as part of a past which is posthumous, as a reminder of the power of the posthumous, and as a reminder that the condition of the present may be that it too is posthumous, and the ghostly afterlife is here already. To this it can be added that film as the medium of the recorded, the completed, is also the medium of the posthumous, where the present seems as ghostly as the past, so that the medium fits with Stanley Kwan's theme.

The revenant in *Rouge* notices the lack of continuity with the past, which, in the film's structure, is interwoven with the present, in a double temporal patterning. *Rouge* comments on Hong Kong's ambivalent relation with its colonial past (the city having no history, or tearing down its history) and with Shanghai, whose culture also survived in ghost-form in Hong Kong after 1949. The culture of the present, summed up in the convenience relationship of the young couple, Ah Chu and Yuen (Emily Chu and Alex Man), contrasts with the passionate love-affair in the brothel. The point of linkage with the past, which gives to these figures of the present a new depth, comes when they find a fragment of a 1930s newspaper which confirms to them the world of the past. Hong Kong in the present has little opportunity to realise its existence as a city full of ghosts, but at the end, the lover who survived is found, old, and a virtual beggar, and, only partially seen through shadows, a virtual ghost, his 'living on' a form of the posthumous. His existence makes Fleur's historical suicide of the 1930s an act out of time, unsuccessful, an incompleted action waiting for a future in the present that can never justify it. *Rouge* sees the energies of the past as baffled and thwarted; centring on women, as ghosts within culture, it also implies the difficulty of that past finding an afterlife.

Shakespeare and Dickens created alternative histories, affirmatory of the nation-state, but while *Rouge* looks back, it makes no investment in that past, even if its act of film-making is one of creating a ghost, doubling the space of the present. From the standpoint of 1987, an ambiguous moment in Hong Kong's sense of its future, ten years before the territory reverted from British to Chinese rule, the need is to create a past, to find a fold within that past in which there might have existed the potential for an other existence that is so palpably not a part of a reading of the present. The figure of the ghost, then, does not present itself, it is evoked by the need in the film-maker, to read the present as though it might contain a ghost within itself.[4] The past is created because the present needs it; the past is needed because the present is dependent upon finding something which is other *within itself,* without which it would be, as the present, nothing but a necropolis. Its afterlife is dependent upon the creation of a past, which means that where the historical past seems to have failed, the present needs to revisit it and to double its own space.

2

From a present which needs to produce a past to give itself an afterlife, I go to another example, of the present being ghosted by both present and future. Perhaps in creating Posthumus, Shakespeare might have known of the claim of his contemporary Ben Jonson that he was 'Posthumous born a moneth after his father's decease' – his father being no bricklayer (as was Jonson's stepfather), but one who 'losed all his estate under Queen Marie, having been cast in prison and forfaited' and 'at last turned Minister'.[5] Perhaps Dickens, a keen actor of Jonson, also knew it. Jonson tries to self-author his life and his afterlife. Around 1604, the year of *Sejanus, His Fall,* which contains in it a Postumus, and numerous vulnerable children who die or are killed after the removal of their fathers, Jonson dropped the letter h from his surname, and so lost the name of the father, and so made himself the more posthumous in making himself autonomous, as if erasing the John that his surname proclaimed him son of. The year 1603 was the time of the loss of Jonson's eldest son, which produced from the posthumous son the verse 'On my First Sonne':

> Farewell, thou child of my right hand and joy;
>   My sinne was too much hope of thee, lov'd boy,
> Seven yeers th'wert lent to me, and I thee pay,
>   Exacted by thy fate, on the just day.
>   O, could I loose all father, now. For why

140

> Will man lament the state he should envie?
> To have so soone scap'd worlds, and fleshes rage,
>   And, if no other miserie, yet age?
> Rest in soft peace, and ask'd, say here doth lye
>   BEN. JONSON his best piece of *poetrie.*
> For whose sake, henceforth, all his vowes be such,
>   As what he loves may never like too much. (*Epigrammes* XLV)

The eldest son is a true Benjamin, 'son of my right hand', the writing hand: the son is poetry. As with the work of Blanchot, the name calls attention to the hand that has written. The posthumous son, BEN. JONSON, who 'lost all father' when he changed the paternal name, has also lost fatherhood in that he has produced poetry that in one sense lies dead, so that it lacks a father, and in another sense is posthumous since the poem lives on (not needing a father). Yet he has not let go (let loose) of paternity, for the poem apostrophises the dead son, while it expects him as the dead son or as the poem to respond: 'ask'd, say here doth lye / BEN. JONSON his best piece of *poetrie*'.

At the same time, these lines are an exercise in becoming posthumous, for in it the dead son – who could be Ben Jonson, or the seven-year-old boy or the poem – points to himself, just as he or it points also to the poem which is his epitaph and in which he lives on and constructs a reader, who has 'ask'd', and who is now also, in relation to the poem's speaking, silenced. Since 'Ben' means 'son' in Hebrew, Ben Jonson memorialises sonship in it (and so the future) twice over, and the name disallows fatherhood (and so the past) twice over, as though this was Jonson's fate. He cannot do anything about the past, or the future. And 'BEN. JONSON his best piece of *poetrie*' is teasing, for the child would have been called Ben Johnson, which means that the patriarch who had changed his name could not control the future in any detail.

'O could I loose all father now' recalls *Cymbeline*'s point that no-one is truly posthumous, because of the power of patriarchy, which here as the second to fourth lines suggest, includes the rule of God as the Father. Nor is David Copperfield outside the power of the father, so that posthumous existence cannot begin. And Nietzsche can only think of his father as dead insofar as he too in his present is posthumous. The past in present modernity is not so easily evaded, which makes an approach to it properly contestatory. Since Jonson, despite having changed his name, remains a father, and cannot 'loose' that status – and commemorates that in a poem – it seems that patriarchy can neither be lost nor its grip loosed; the enduring patriarchalism of the poem also, unconsciously, shows itself in the entire occlusion of the mother from any part in the relationship with the son. The element of self-fashioning or self-authorisation is itself patriarchal. To 'loose' all father, which would make the subject posthumous (having no father) and the next generation posthumous (because he as father had dissolved his identity), would suggest that the power of the posthumous cannot be brought about from the standpoint of the present. The present cannot free itself from the past, even if it neglects or repudiates that past. That freedom can only come about from the past, or, as Jonson expresses it in the desire to 'loose all father', from the present's relationship to the future.

If the freedom from the past can only come about from the past, this is another example of a fact becoming historical posthumously. The present establishes the past, but the past that is established must not be commanding: indeed it is a created past, and not created as source or as father, which means it cannot have the power to be commanding in the present. The language of 'heritage' as applied to history-become-tourism is the reverse; thinking of the past as patriarchal, it implicitly accords to the present the right to think of itself as able to do what it likes with its heritage (we have inherited the heritage), which can be conceptualised in terms which define the inheritance by material successfulness, to be appropriated for profit.

3

Though the past seems to produce the present, the singularity of any event breaks with that sequencing, and nothing in the present can be quite accounted for by the past, which is why Wordsworth in *The Prelude* calls the Imagination 'an unfather'd vapour' (1805 version, VI.527). Wordsworth writes that phrase in

1804, fourteen years after the experience of crossing the Alps, about which he was writing, so that even the experience of the Alps does not father the perception of the Imagination. The Imagination is out of time, and apocalyptic, so that a few lines further on, Wordsworth reads the Alpine scenery as 'Characters of the great Apocalypse, / The types and symbols of Eternity' (VI.570–1). The Alps lose their place in the present, as guarantors of an enduring Nature, and intimate the presence of the catastrophic. Fear of the apocalyptic has already been anticipated in *The Prelude* V – 'Books', when, in a dream, the Arab is seen hastening to bury the books that he fears will be engulfed by waters. For one of the books, in its dream-appearance as a shell, a husk, a relic of a life that has departed, foretells 'destruction to the Children of the Earth / By deluge now at hand' (V.98–9). The book, then, both announces time and the presence of the apocalypse. Burying the books, which represent the power of the past, is an act to preserve them, as well as a way of renouncing authority over them or renouncing their authority over the present and the future, their power to create an afterlife – and to do that by pronouncing their death, declaring them to be funerary in character, so that their existence is now to be posthumous, and the book which prophesies disaster will not be able to bring it about. The catastrophe is imminent; unless the books are buried, the books *will* be buried in the flood. Unless some action is taken with regard to the texts of the past, which have their own destructive patriarchal potential, such texts will be rendered unreadable. The section ends with an identification with the mad Arab, who in the double life of the dream is also Don Quixote, maddened by reading the books without which the world is wholly disenchanted:

> yea, I will say,
> In sober contemplation of the approach
> Of such great overthrow, made manifest
> By certain evidence, that I, methinks,
> Could share that Maniac's anxiousness, could go
> Upon like errand. Oftentimes at least
> Me hath such deep entrancement half-possess'd
> When I have held a volume in my hand
> Poor earthly casket of immortal Verse!
> Shakespeare, or Milton, Labourers divine! (V.156–65)

Fear of the end of history, of the apocalyptic, which is also fear of what the present contains, makes the poet manic, fearing both that what is past will have no further existence, and also that 'the book will engulf, entomb, both us and the sea'.[6] This seems to me to describe an urgent double demand within literary and cultural studies. Such awareness, which makes the apocalyptic part of history, not separate from it (so, to take another form of apocalypse than drowning, if there is to be book-burning, then it is the culture of the book that has brought this about), requires taking 'Poor earthly casket of immortal Verse' to mean that 'the book is the mortal continuance of immortal verse; on the other hand, the book is an earthly casket *made up of*, constituted by, immortal verse – in short, the verses *are* the casket, in which case their immortality is that of a coffin'.

4

In *Rouge* there is the power of an unappeased past, in Jonson the desire to be free of the past, in Wordsworth fear of the future annihilating the past *and* the past containing the annihilation of the present and future. For the German critic Erich Auerbach, the concept of *figura* emphasised the importance of the 'after-life' of events, showing that an event is never finished, but that it continues to accrete further significance, *increasing* reality within its afterlife. According to Auerbach, figural interpretation of the Bible, or of Dante

> establishes a connection between two events or persons in such a way that the first signifies not only itself but also the second, while the second involves or fulfills the first. The two events of a figure are separated in time, but both, being real events or persons, are within temporality.

Figural interpretation can be extended, within a schema which reads history in terms of divine providence, by taking 'the sacrifice of Isaac . . . as prefiguring the sacrifice of Christ'.[7] Figural interpretation, within Dante's *Commedia*, may start with the *Inferno*, canto X of which, the episode of Farinata and Cavalcante,

Auerbach discusses in *Mimesis*. Here, it should be noted, that in the *Commedia*, virtually all the figures are posthumous – there are virtually *no* live people to be found in any of its parts, *Inferno*, *Purgatorio* or *Paradiso*; Dante walks among ghosts whose passion is still for the present on earth. The ghostly figures of the *Inferno* continue to hurt themselves and to be hurt and to recall their griefs, and are brought into a fuller subjectivity, as is the ghost in *Rouge*. The afterlife is not less real than the events which are their shadow; it is, indeed, more intense. The threat within the 'afterlife' is to make the 'events' disappear, making them instead textual traces. Thus Auerbach finds Dante's realism to appear in a more pronounced mode in dealing with souls who are beyond the tomb, who, in this specific case, had denied the existence of an afterlife, which makes their adherence to their mode of life on earth more poignant.

Auerbach's critique of Dante has been decisive in showing how a more intense posthumous existence calls into question any possibility of assigning to any character a fate, or settling his or her afterlife for ever; energies once set in motion continue on the basis of death, not despite it. Yet, while paying that due to Auerbach, it is yet worth noting how Levinas, in *Difficult Freedom* criticises the concept of *figura*: that such an idea of the present figuring something whose reality will become apparent in the future neglects the present and engagement with the face of the other, who now only prefigures something else. The Old Testament is killed off by the omnipresence of figural interpretation, where incidents are only permitted to prefigure later events.[8] The question for Dante criticism would be how to read posthumous encounters as present, and in that way to meet the face of the other. Another way of coming at that point would be to compare Auerbach with Benjamin's sense of history, which rejects development. *Figura* allows for no entropy, proposing rather that an action in the present is completed in the future; hence the greater reality with which Farinata and Cavalcante are seen when dead. The logic of Auerbach's 'mimesis' proposes that 'history itself is mimesis, the representation of the dead past'. History as writing the past 'must always' – on the basis of figural realism – 'reduce history as an ontological object into a dead letter, so that it might be "meaningful", the literal sign for an allegorical meaning'.[9] Auerbach's model is linear, requiring that an event in the future repeats the past with a fuller intensity, but, nonetheless, as the return of the same. It is uncoincidental that Auerbach's chosen model for interpretation is *Inferno*, for this is the place which his analysis has encouraged the reading that accepts that the present must pay for the past (the reverse of Nietzsche's emphasis in *Zarathustra*), so that in it present emotions follow a past line of action, which includes a sense that past modes of inscription are repeated with more intensity in the present. Is there no way to escape from a past inscription of character? Is the afterlife to be the same as the past life?

Posthumus says of the allegorical writing laid upon him in prison that 'the action of my life is like it' (*Cymbeline*, V, iv, 150). Keats said of Shakespeare (letter, 18 February 1819) that Shakespeare 'led a life of allegory: his works are the comments on it'. Keats's sense of allegory may perhaps be distinguished from the romantic symbol, for a 'life of allegory' might imply an awareness that no connections can be made between the life's fragmented parts – as with Nietzsche's existence – which does not resolve into that of a single identity, so that Shakespeare's plays relate to fragments that cannot be established in a diachronic relationship. The subject does not know the contents of his or her life. Posthumus accepts the fragmented existence of the writing and does not interpret it; interpretation belongs rather to the Soothsayer, whose profession is, as always with soothsayers, to foretell a future marked by continuity, of unending upward lines on graphs, undisturbed by the apocalyptic, the future validating present policy.

5

In his essay 'The Task of the Translator' (1924) Walter Benjamin considers that the translation of a text may not be as 'good' as the original, but that translation confers upon the text an afterlife. 'The text has a life, and an afterlife [*Überleben*, its survival, its living on]'. The text's living on in its original form is posthumous, in that it survives the occasion of its making, but then, as 'a translation comes later than the original, and since the important works of world literature never find their chosen translators at the time of their origin, their translation marks their stage of continued life [*Fortleben*]'. Translation, then, works upon the posthumous, and by doing so releases the text into a new form of existence. We could say that Ben Jonson's son and his poem were both translations, translations of each other, continuing desires for an afterlife. Benjamin continues:

> It is the task of the translator to release in his own language the pure language which is under the spell of another, to liberate the language imprisoned in a work in his re-creation of that work. (*Illuminations*, 71, 80)

Translation may not 'better' an original, but it also shows up the original text in its language to be repressed, caught in a language and signifying system (for example, attached to nationhood and a national literature, attached to views about gender or race or class) from which it needs to be released. The 'afterlife' of the text becomes *more* important than its life. As Jonson's best piece of poetry reflects upon the need of the author, whose surrender of his autonomy as poet is signalled in the words 'O could I loose all father, now' (he contemplates losing his existence as a poet fathering poetry, and his existence as a patriarch), so translation becomes a necessary way in which the past text speaks again, however posthumous, and as translated.

A little earlier, in 1921, writing on Goethe's *Elective Affinities*, Benjamin had dwelt on the role of critique, which 'seeks the truth content of a work of art', as distinct from 'commentary', which seeks 'its material content'. The truth content is bound to the material content, its subject-matter, 'inconspicuously' and 'intimately' but as Michael Jennings phrases it, Benjamin

> reads the work of art as a self-consuming process within history. As historical distance increases, the importance of specific content for understanding the work decreases, permitting the work's truth content to emerge all the more clearly.[10]

The truth content is hidden, but appears in fragmentary form as the work passes into history, into its afterlife, as the union of truth and subject-matter fall apart. The critic is like a palaeographer 'in front of a parchment whose faded text is covered by the lineaments of a more powerful script which refers to that text. As the palaeographer would have to begin by reading the latter script, the critic would have to begin with commentary.' To see these two scripts as separate, to recognise that there is something palimpsest-like below the surface, is the work of the text's afterlife: 'the history of works prepares for their critique, and thus historical distance increases their power'.[11]

The life of the work depends on a posthumous existence, which is again demonstrated in translation, which radically and necessarily changes the 'material content'. Usually criticism (which is really 'commentary') keeps working on the material content, justifying it, idealising it, resolving everything into the richly symbolic, as Benjamin felt had happened to *Elective Affinities*, and as happens with criticism of the *Commedia*, but critique brings out something else, which gives the text its after-life. Further on, Benjamin uses the term the 'expressionless', which for him dismantles the fluent expressivity of the novel (part of its material content):

> The expressionless is the critical violence which, while unable to separate semblance from essence in art, prevents them from mingling. It possesses this violence as a moral dictum. In the expressionless, the sublime violence of the true appears as that which determines the language of the real world according to the laws of the moral world. For it shatters whatever still survives as the legacy of chaos in all beautiful semblance: the false, errant totality – the absolute totality. Only the expressionless completes the work, by shattering it into a thing of shards, into a fragment of the true world, into the torso of a symbol. As a category of language and art and not of the work or of the genres, the expressionless can no more be rigorously defined than through a passage in Hölderlin's . . . 'Annotations to Oedipus' . . . The passage reads: 'For the tragic transport is actually empty and the least restrained. – Thereby, in the rhythmic sequence of the representations wherein the transport shows itself, there becomes necessary what in poetic metre is called caesura, the pure word, the counter-rhythmic rupture – namely, in order to meet the onrushing change of representations at its highest point, in such a manner that not the change of representation but the representation itself very soon appears. ('Goethe's *Elective Affinities*', 340–1)

Hölderlin on the caesura has already been quoted (see above, pp. 113–14). The caesura – where 'every expression simultaneously comes to a standstill' (341) – breaks the appearance of a 'natural order' within the text, a natural progression, identifiable with history as progress. It reveals this as not natural, but as part of the world of representation (i.e. as ideology). The caesura appears within the text's afterlife, and it turns the text from its appearance of giving the 'totality', towards being seen as 'the torso of a symbol'. Again, this afterlife may be related to translation. Paul de Man writing on 'The Task of the Translator' sees the translation as a fragment, and emphasises that the original and the translation do not add together to make up a whole.[12] They may be articulated together, but a translation points to the work of art of which it is the signifier. The translation becomes an allegory of the work in the past, a fragment pointing to something whose nature is posthumous, since only an act of translation can make it survive. The afterlife as allegory describes a posthumous state. As 'events' are not the dynamic acts of an immediate present, so the present is a moment incomplete in itself (hence the caesura within it), pointing to something else, just as any work in the past also points beyond itself to those precursor texts which it calls into significance.

Translation removes a text from a past and a tradition, and does an analogous work to what Benjamin sees technology doing for the work of art, since

> the technique of reproduction detaches the reproduced object from the domain of tradition. By making many reproductions it substitutes a plurality of copies for a unique existence. In permitting the reproduction to meet the beholder or listener in his own particular situation, it reactivates the object reproduced. These two processes lead to a tremendous shattering of tradition which is the obverse of the contemporary crisis and renewal of mankind. (*Illuminations*, 223)

As part of tradition, the work is confirmed as dead, part of a 'cultural heritage', but its existence in an afterlife makes its past historical. As reproduced, it is not the 'original' but its present existence in the form it possesses – a form whose success in being what it is is obviously open to question – gives it an allegorical quality. Two moments are laid open; the past text speaks differently from its place inside a tradition and a history.

6

Paris change! mais rien dans ma mélancolie
N'a bougé! palais neufs, échafaudages, blocs,
Vieux faubourgs, tout pour moi devient allégorie,
Et mes chers souvenirs sont plus lourds que des rocs.[13]

Baudelaire's 'Le Cygne' comes from the moment when the old Paris had virtually disappeared under the aggressive restructurings and modernisation of Baron Haussmann in the 1850s, a present of empty monumentalism signifying 'Paris' replacing an older historical city, and leading to a feeling that what is to be seen is not what matters; as the ghost in *Rouge* knows, the form, or the face, of a city changes faster than the heart of a mortal.[14] Modernity evokes memory, as it also evokes melancholia, where nothing of the past has budged. As buildings in the nineteenth-century were torn down, replaced by others in a state which made Paris as the modern urban scene a perpetual construction-site, everything for Baudelaire became allegory – fragmented, not to be read literally, the space of an absence in itself. The city will not be 'nice when it's finished', as is often said of Hong Kong, for that, if it was possible, would *finish off* an afterlife set up by the past. Rather, the present city's empty signifiers and its mode of coming into being allegorise the past city, and a past temporality which was never complete either. As Paris has been torn down and as scaffolding proclaims that it is being rebuilt, modernity is marked by a temporal rupture with the past, and its buildings allegorise this break; they allegorise in other words, lack of continuity with the past, which means that the past can only be brought back as a fragment, as a ruin, as allegory.[15]

The new city enables the past city to be seen posthumously through the power of allegory. A current fashion in writing about London in contrast thinks of the city in terms of continuity marked by a psychogeography – where, over different historical periods, similar forms of behaviour are noted within specific areas, as though each area harbours its own ghost.[16] This seems a sentimentalism whose interest is in preserving the past (selectively, nostalgically, forgetting the difference of the present), as though the past was in danger of being lost; similarly its determinism refuses the possibility of continuity: everything has stopped already and there is no way to go but back to the past. Baudelaire's sense of the modern present reverses that. Past ghosts are generated by the present, their unappeased existence emphasised by the effort of the present to become what it can hardly be – present; since the past is in the present and present temporal ruptures could never happen if the present, as something desired, could be brought into single existence.

Notes

1. Reinhardt Koselleck, *Futures Past: On the Semantics of Historical Time*, trans. Keith Tribe (Cambridge, MA: MIT Press, 1985), p. 250.
2. On this film, Ackbar Abbas, *Hong Kong: Culture and the Politics of Disappearance* (Minneapolis: University of Minnesota Press, 1997), pp. 39–44; Fredric Jameson, *The Cultural Turn: Selected Writings on the Postmodern, 1983–1998* (London: Verso, 1998), pp. 188–9; Lisa Odham Stokes and Michael Hoover, *City on Fire: Hong Kong Cinema* (London: Verso, 1999), pp. 161–4; Leo Ou-fan Lee, *Shanghai Modern* (Cambridge, MA: Harvard University Press, 1999), pp. 335–6.
3. Jean Baudrillard, *Symbolic Exchange and Death*, trans. Hugh Hamilton Grant (London: SAGE, 1993), pp. 185–6. For the Benjamin quotation, see *Illuminations*, p. 244.
4. I have explored this theme in Henry James: his need to produce an American past, to make new ghosts walk whose habitat was within that past. Jeremy Tambling, *Henry James: Critical Issues* (London: Macmillan, 2000).
5. Quoted, David Riggs, *Ben Jonson: A Life* (Cambridge, MA: Harvard University Press, 1989), p. 9.
6. This, and the next quotation come from Andrzej Warminski, 'Missed Crossing: Wordsworth's Apocalypses', *Modern Language Notes* 99 (1984), 983–1005, p. 1005. See also on this passage J. Hillis Miller, *The Linguistic Moment: From Wordsworth to Stevens* (Princeton: Princeton University Press, 1985), pp. 59–113. A nice coincidence makes Hillis Miller's last poetic example Stevens, author of the *Opus Posthumous*

(1957). Miller on Wordsworth writes 'each poem is implicitly posthumous, and presupposes the vanishing of its author' (108).

7. Erich Auerbach, *Mimesis*, trans. Willard Trask (New York: Doubleday Anchor, 1957), p. 64. See also p. 170 for application to Dante. The essay *'Figura'* appears in Auerbach's *Scenes from the Drama of European Literature*, trans. Ralph Manheim (Chicago: University of Chicago Press, 1959). See Alan Charity's *Events and their Afterlife* (Cambridge: Cambridge University Press, 1966) for an application of Auerbach.

8. See Jill Robbins, *Altered Reading: Levinas and Literature* (Chicago: University of Chicago Press, 1999), pp. 42, 46.

9. Timorthy Bahti, 'Auerbach's *Mimesis*: Figural Structure and Historical Narrative', in Gregory S. Jay and David L. Miller (eds), *After Strange Texts: The Role of Theory in the Study of Literature* (Alabama: University of Alabama Press, 1985), pp. 124–45, p. 145. I bring Benjamin into relation with Dante in 'Dante and Benjamin: Allegory and Melancholy', *Exemplaria* 4.2 (1992), 341–63. Jesse Gellrich idealises *figura* in his comparison with Benjamin's allegory, which he takes as a marker of exhaustion, in his *'Figura*, Allegory and the Question of History', in Seth Lerer (ed.), *Literary History and the Challenge of Philology* (Stanford: Stanford University Press, 1996), pp. 107–23.

10. Michael W. Jennings, *Dialectical Images: Walter Benjamin's Theory of Literary Criticism* (Ithaca: Cornell University Press, 1987), p. 129.

11. *Walter Benjamin: Selected Writings vol. 1: 1913–1926*, ed. Marcus Bullock and Michael W. Jennings (Cambridge, MA: Harvard University Press, 1996), pp. 297–8. Translation by Stanley Corngold. The translation in the Introduction to *Illuminations* (pp. 4–5) is worth comparing with this.

12. Paul de Man, *The Resistance to Theory* (Minneapolis: University of Minnesota Press, 1986), pp. 90–1.

13. Baudelaire, 'Le Cygne', *Les Fleurs du Mal*, LXXXIX . 'Paris changes! But nothing in my melancholy has changed. New palaces, scaffolds, blocks, old neighbourhoods, everything for me becomes allegory, and my dear memories are heavier than rocks.'

14. 'Le vieux Paris n'est plus (la forme d'une ville / Change plus vite, hélas! que le coeur d'un mortel)' – 'Le Cygne'.
15. On this, see Ross Chambers, *The Writing of Melancholy: Modes of Opposition in Early French Modernism*, trans. Mary Seidman Trouille (Chicago: University of Chicago Press, 1993), pp. 153–73.
16. See, for example, Peter Ackroyd, *London: The Biography* (London: Chatto and Windus, 2000); the title suggests the organicist approach taken, presupposing a single history, and, presumably, a finished life; see also the review by Phil Baker, 'The Bellringer of Lost London', *TLS* 24 November 2000, p. 14. The organicist sense in Ackroyd, his insistence on the presence, means that in his novel *Chatterton* (New York: Grove Press, 1987) he cannot notice that Chatterton was posthumous.

Index